ACCEPTANCE AND COMMITMENT THERAPY FOR ANXIETY RELIEF

ACCEPTANCE *and* COMMITMENT THERAPY *for* ANXIETY RELIEF

How to Evolve Your Relationship with Your Mind

Rachel Willimott, LCSW

ROCKRIDGE
PRESS

Interior and Cover Designer: Regina Stadnik
Art Producer: Meg Baggott
Editor: Shannon Criss / Adrian Potts
Production Editor: Jenna Dutton

Author photo courtesy of Morgan Alanna Photography

ISBN: Print 978-1-64739-864-4 | eBook 978-1-64739-542-1
R0

To my clients:
Thank you for letting me into your lives.
May you all experience freedom.

Contents

Introduction

Welcome! I am so glad you are here. I have so much passion for both Acceptance and Commitment Therapy (abbreviated as ACT and said as one word, i.e., "act") and working with anxiety. I hope that the skills I describe in this book will be helpful to you.

I am Rachel Willimott, a licensed clinical social worker. I learned of ACT as an undergraduate student at the University of Nevada, Reno, where ACT originator Dr. Steven C. Hayes is a professor and researcher. I participated in a research study for ACT my first year in college, during which a licensed psychologist taught the skills one semester. I wish I could say that I instantly fell in love with ACT, but I actually struggled with the skills at first. To me, it was not intuitive to take my mind less seriously and sit with difficult emotions. I stayed the course, though, and found real change with ACT.

I have worked as a therapist since 2015, developing my understanding of ACT through formal ACT training, working closely with other ACT therapists, reading every book I can find on ACT, and using it in my work with clients every day. ACT is more than just a therapy; it is a worldview and a way of looking at suffering and healing. It has been transformative in my own life, and I have seen it transform others' lives as well.

Working with all the ways anxiety appears has become a passion of mine. On one end of the anxiety spectrum, I have worked with professionals with relationships and careers who have an uneasy sense of not belonging or of imminent failure. On the other side are my clients with severe trauma histories, and those who struggle to leave their home even to attend therapy. The same types of suffering can be found, and the same steps of healing can be used through it all.

Reading this book and completing the exercises will help you develop an understanding of the processes of anxiety, as well as psychological flexibility processes—the very skills taught in ACT.

This knowledge will allow you to practice skills that help you work with anxiety in a different way and take the necessary steps to having the life you want. You will see the science behind ACT throughout the book, as well as how it has helped others.

I will return to the following key point throughout this book: ACT will not eliminate the experience of fear and anxiety. Rather, it will give you your life back and empower you to do the things you have avoided due to anxiety. Relief from anxiety means that while anxiety will occasionally be present in your life, more importantly, *you* will become present in your life. ACT skills provide relief from the struggle we have against our own minds. Using ACT in my own life has allowed me to move to a new city; launch a business; have painful, honest conversations with people I care about; and, ultimately, be my authentic self. I have experienced self-doubt, fear, and anxiety throughout these experiences, but ACT has allowed me to "act" even when these feelings showed up, and to have compassion for myself and others along the way.

I hope for the same for you.

Getting Started

Chapter 1 will help you understand the background behind the many forms of anxiety. In chapter 2, I will describe ACT itself, the robust science behind it, and how it helps with anxiety. Chapters 3 through 8 will each focus on one ACT process, teaching you skills to practice and exercises to implement. Each chapter builds off the last, so I recommend reading in order. Throughout the book, I use case studies and examples from my work to illustrate how the skills have worked in practice. Please know that names and details have been changed to protect the privacy of those involved, but the experience of the skills remains.

If you want to see real change in your life, the strongest recommendation I can make is to practice each skill daily. You might choose to read this book slowly, practicing each skill for a few days before moving on. You might also choose to move through this book more quickly, practicing multiple skills daily. In my own work, I have noticed that when I do skills in session and clients practice them between sessions, there is rapid progress. When we just talk about the skills, or a client does not practice them between sessions, progress stagnates.

It can be helpful to schedule time in your day or week to read a chapter, the same way clients schedule therapy appointments. Some exercises require a journal to complete, so it can be very beneficial to have a dedicated space to note your progress and your experience with each skill, as well as work through the exercises. Then, choose times throughout the day to practice the skills. For some, following the provided times and places to practice is ideal, and for others, using your own schedule and intuition to find times to practice will work better. The goal is for these skills to be easily accessible for you whenever you begin to struggle with anxiety. These skills are not like antibiotics; you will not do a course of them and then be done. Nor are they like a shot of epinephrine, only for use in moments of crisis. Instead, they are like exercise or sleeping—you do them every day to continue living your best life.

Once you know all six processes (or skills) of ACT, you will be able to use them fluidly. It is a bit like riding a bike. In this book you will learn the mechanics of riding the "bike" of ACT, and start trying it out in your own life. By the end, you will remove the training wheels and start riding the bike every day on your own. While the skills are taught sequentially to help you learn them individually, they are a complete package for your life.

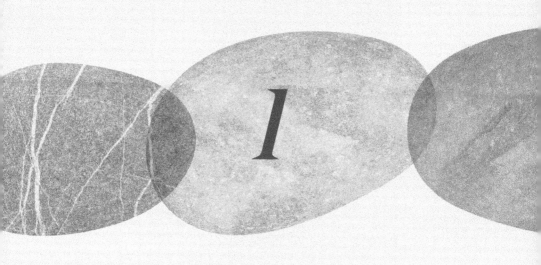

1

UNDERSTANDING ANXIETY

A full, rich life includes fear and anxiety. Many animals also experience fear. I need only to witness my dog's frightened response to a snowman to know that she experiences this feeling. For humans, this fear extends from the present moment into the past and future. Our incredible capacity for language allows us to make cities, understand the cosmos, and express ourselves through art. It also allows our minds to imagine tomorrow's meeting going poorly, worry about the health of our families, and ponder our own mortality.

Anxiety becomes a problem when we take our mind's rules and problem solving literally, and when our responses to anxiety stop us from living a full life. Throughout this book, we will dissect the ways our ability to problem solve becomes a hindrance. This chapter examines the different forms of anxiety, factors—including biological and environmental—that lead to anxiety problems, and how anxiety shows up in our brains and bodies.

Trauma

Anxiety Disorder Classifications

Experiencing fear and anxiety is part of being human, but our reactions to it can become a problem. Genetics are only a tiny factor in mental health diagnoses. In fact, someone with a biological tendency toward vigilance may not develop an anxiety disorder if they are raised with a nurturing family that models psychological flexibility—the very skills you will learn here! However, many of us learn to avoid or suppress our experience and sadly, some were raised in neglectful or even abusive homes. All these factors can lead to anxiety disorders. The National Comorbidity Survey Replication, a comprehensive survey about mental health in the United States, found that nearly a third of us will struggle with an anxiety condition at some point in our lives.

Before we examine the various types of anxiety, I want to define mental health disorders. First, they are not diseases. A disease has a cause, follows a course, and responds predictably to treatment. Mental health disorders do not fit that criteria. Instead, they are clusters of symptoms, and people are diagnosed when they meet more than half the criteria.

Acceptance and Commitment Therapy (ACT) views mental health problems, and all human suffering, as stemming from normal processes. Although the traditional diagnostic system uses the term "disorder" to identify "that which deviates from the norm," we contend in ACT that suffering is the norm. ACT is a process-based approach, so I will speak to the underlying processes of each diagnosis.

Generalized Anxiety Disorder

Generalized anxiety disorder, or GAD, is characterized by uncontrollable worry about a variety of events, along with at least half of the following symptoms: restlessness, fatigue, difficulty concentrating, irritability, muscle tension, or sleep problems. People often report having these experiences for most of their lives before seeking treatment; many people initially talk to their primary care physician about the symptoms because so many of them are physical.

People with anxiety and GAD tend to react to normal experiences like worry or anxiety with self-criticism and judgment. Imagine worrying about the future of your job, thinking "I can't think like this! I must stay calm. What is wrong with me? Why do I worry so much?" Now you are worrying about worry, and these judgments only fuel the anxiety.

Two important mental processes explain much of human suffering. **Fusion**—or taking thoughts literally and allowing them to control our behavior—is one process that leads to anxiety disorders. Subconscious or implicit rules are part of fusion, and might sound like:

- Uncertainty is intolerable.
- Having a plan will make me feel better.
- Feeling good is my primary goal.

The other process—**experiential avoidance**/or avoiding our own internal experience—includes trying to control the worry and anxiety. Some examples include:

- Suppressing thoughts
- Seeking reassurance
- Procrastinating or overpreparing

Even when people are actively engaged in their lives, they might not be present or focused; instead, they are thinking of the next worst-case scenario. Experiential avoidance can also look like avoiding joy or hope because they feel too vulnerable.

The avoidance process also appears in GAD, in the use of worry to manage fear associated with visual thoughts. Because worry is a more abstract thought, it can function as avoidance of more painful, visual thoughts.

For example, Sasha was incredibly anxious about getting evicted from her apartment. She had adopted a dog that she later realized exceeded weight restrictions. She described having an intrusive image of coming home to an eviction notice on her door. Her stomach would drop at this image, then her mind launched into problem solving: "I can tell them I am sorry. I could negotiate a move-out deal to avoid an eviction on my record," and on and on it went. Sasha would spend minutes, sometimes nearly an hour, spinning her wheels on a problem that was not currently happening, just to avoid the pain of that image that lasted only seconds. The images would not go away, thus reinforcing the loop.

Six months later, Sasha moved out, having never heard from management. She prepared for an event that never occurred, missing out on experiencing the present of many days during this period.

GAD is often considered the prototype of all other anxiety disorders; to manage and control our sense of anxiety, we prepare for any and all negative possibilities. This behavior takes us out of our present life and goals, and it usually isn't even that effective. Anyone who has mentally rehearsed an argument that never happened can confirm our minds' inability to accurately predict the future.

Social Anxiety

Many people experience nervousness at giving a presentation, speaking to a group, or meeting someone new. Some of us may prefer having more alone time and a smaller cluster of close friends—a trait often referred to as introversion.

Neither of these feelings and preferences is social anxiety, however. Social anxiety is characterized by a persistent and intense fear surrounding social situations, such as having conversations or meeting new people, being observed when eating or drinking, or performing in front of others. People who meet the criteria for social anxiety also worry that their fear will be "found out," that others around will know that they are anxious. This fear leads to avoidance or fearful endurance of social situations.

With many people first experiencing social anxiety symptoms in childhood and early adolescence, this pattern of fear and avoidance leads many to not marry, complete higher education, or maintain a job. As we saw with GAD, the understandable desire to avoid pain becomes the problem.

Specific Phobias

Specific phobias are characterized by an immediate, out-of-proportion fear, along with avoidance or fearful endurance, of a specific object or situation. These can include heights, driving, animals, or needles, among others. The phobia may be linked to a specific experience or may have no apparent origin. In fact, research begun by Martin Seligman in 1971 and continued by ACT researchers into the present day have found that some common phobias—such as heights, snakes, spiders, and thunderstorms—have an evolutionary advantage. Fear of these objects and situations likely kept our ancestors safe. These phobias are also faster to acquire than phobias of more modern objects, such as guns. Regardless of the type of phobia, people struggle to tolerate the feeling of fear and act in ways to avoid it. This can include relatively small methods, such as taking a different route home, to life-changing methods, such as turning down a great job because it is in a city with a lot of bridges.

Panic Disorder

A panic attack is a surge of intense fear that peaks in minutes. Symptoms may include rapid heart rate; sweating; shaking; choking or an out-of-breath sensation; chest pain; nausea; feeling dizzy or faint; chills or feeling overheated; numbness or tingling; a sense of being detached from oneself or reality; or a fear of going crazy or dying. While intense fear is a response to a threat, whether in reality or imagined, panic attacks often are not associated with a cue. About a third of young adults have a panic attack in any given year, and only a fraction of this group will go on to fit criteria for panic disorder.

The worry of having additional panic attacks or how the panic attacks will affect the person's life differentiates the experience of panic attacks from the condition of panic disorder. The fear of feeling fear is the problem. Intolerance of the experience of panic or fear, including the physical sensations associated with panic, leads to increased fear of having a panic attack, which leads to avoiding anything that could trigger fear. In fact, breathing techniques, once thought to be helpful to panic disorder, can worsen it if they are used to control anxiety.

The use of avoidance can lead to a separate (but related) disorder called agoraphobia. This is essentially the fear and avoidance of being stuck in a situation without help or an escape. Situations that people with agoraphobia might avoid include movie theaters, malls, driving away from home, or crowds. Again, it is not a phobia of these locations, but what they represent: the inability to flee if panic shows up.

ANXIETY IN OTHER CONDITIONS

You may have noticed a theme in my description of common anxiety disorders: anxiety becomes disordered when our relationship to our thoughts, feelings, and bodily sensations causes us to avoid any anxiety trigger. This same process underlies other mental health conditions, including obsessive-compulsive disorder (OCD) and post-traumatic stress disorder (PTSD), neither of which are catalogued with anxiety disorders.

OCD is characterized by intrusive, upsetting thoughts, along with behaviors to minimize these thoughts. A person may have an image of hurting someone else, then feel the intense urge to recite a prayer several times to extinguish the thought. Another may have a recurring thought that they will make their family sick, and need to wash their hands several times or avoid a part of their house to prevent this. The process is the same: Anxiety and thoughts become something to vanquish, and the efforts to do so end up taking over the person's life.

PTSD is unique in that it requires a cause: an experience that made you feel like you might die or be harmed, or repeatedly hearing of similar experiences. The power of our minds can make thinking about a terrifying event a trigger for the same emotions at similar intensities as the original experience. Memories can feel like we are reliving the terror all over again. If someone begins avoiding that experience, they can get caught in a loop of intrusive memories and avoidance, feeling intense emotions and numbness all at once.

THE FOLLOWING CASE STUDY DEMONSTRATES THE BLURRY LINES BETWEEN ANXIETY DISORDERS

Charlie had a fear of traveling. He had had a traumatic experience of being forgotten at the gas station when he was younger, and then, as a teenager, he had a panic attack in a car. Since then, he had become fearful of moving outside a tight radius of home and work, regardless of transportation method.

When we discussed his fear, Charlie said he was not afraid of getting hurt; he was afraid of having a panic attack. You might see possible connections here to PTSD, panic disorder, agoraphobia, and specific driving phobia. Instead of focusing on the specific diagnosis, I looked at the processes. Charlie's fear of experiencing fear led him to avoid any trigger, reinforcing thoughts that he could not handle traveling, and ultimately limiting his life.

Mind and Body Connection

Before we dive into the physical and mental effects of anxiety, I'd like to note the difference between anxiety and fear. Fear is an emotion that responds to an external event happening in the present. When our brains register a threat, the fight-or-flight response kicks in, characterized by increased sweating; rapid heart rate; higher blood pressure; labored breathing; a narrowing of attention; and an urge to fight, get away from the situation, or freeze in place. If this response fits the circumstances, it is serving its biological purpose of allowing us to get to safety. For our primate relatives, this response happens when a predator or rival primate is near. Humans can transfer that response to social rejection, the idea of our own mortality, or a nightmare. Conversely, anxiety is a response to internal experiences and thoughts, such as uncertainty or possible future events.

Although fear and anxiety have their evolutionary benefits, such as keeping us alive when danger is near or helping us plan for the future, chronic stress and anxiety have costly effects on our well-being. You might think of the relationship between anxiety and our minds and bodies as that of a complex ecosystem: One change to the system can trickle down and affect the rest of the system in surprising ways. Chronic stress, whether external life stressors or the stress of panic and worry, can lead to additional problems such as muscle tension; cardiovascular, respiratory, and digestive issues; sexual and reproductive health difficulties; and other mental health problems. Factors like childhood trauma, stress in the family, and genetics can make those ill effects more likely. Even the experiences of our family members can affect our resiliency to anxiety.

Generational trauma can be genetically passed down (e.g., it's been shown that grandchildren of Holocaust survivors have genetic markers indicating increased vigilance to stress). Therefore, we carry the history of our families in our bodies. Research in the science of epigenetics has found that our experiences can further affect how genes are expressed. For example, a gene can predict more depression or less depression, depending on life experience. The wonderful news is that learning psychological flexibility skills taught in ACT can modulate some of those reactions, thus actually changing the way the brain works. When the brain is not constantly scanning for danger and negativity, you have more energy and attention to focus on what is important to you.

Muscle tension is a more short-term response to fear. Our muscles automatically tense up when we are exposed to a threat. When this reaction is part of normal, transitory fear, our muscles relax again. However, when we are exposed to chronic stress, whether from external events or the constant stress of vigilance and worry predominant in anxiety disorders, our muscles have no opportunity to relax. This leads to chronic muscle tension, which can be felt in the lower back or upper body. Chronic muscle tension in the shoulders and neck can also lead to tension headaches and migraines.

Chronic stress can affect the cardiovascular system. As discussed above, momentary fear leads to a rapid heart rate and higher blood pressure, allowing blood to quickly circulate to large muscles and the heart, which is necessary for us to use muscles to fight or flee. However, if this process is engaged frequently, there is higher risk for heart problems, including a heart attack. Chronic stress also impacts the immune system, which can lead to chronic fatigue and immune disorders.

Anxiety can also impact the **respiratory system**. Panic attacks and anxiety do not *cause* breathing issues, although when people often fear that they will not be able to breathe in the middle of a panic attack, they can exacerbate conditions like asthma. Rapid breathing during stress can also lead to hyperventilation, which, in turn, can lead to a panic attack for those already prone to them. These actions create a vicious cycle of stress, panic, and worrying about panic.

Many people first seek treatment for their anxiety through their primary care doctor. A common complaint is **digestive issues**. Many of the people I have worked with who have experienced anxiety have also reported digestive issues like frequent nausea, lack of appetite, constipation, or diarrhea. There is a link between the brain and cells in the stomach, which explains why we often experience fear in our guts. Chronic stress can lead to the stomach problems many people report. It can also change the nature of gut bacteria, which influences our moods.

Finally, chronic stress can impact **reproduction and sexual health**. In men, chronic stress can lead to changes in testosterone, reduced sex drive, and reduced ability to conceive. Similarly, stress can affect the entire female reproduction cycle. For women carrying many roles and responsibilities, a reduced sex drive can be one of the many difficulties they experience. Working to avoid and control anxiety also takes us out of the present, and being present is essential to a healthy sex life. Finally, many people find that their anxiety disorder behaviors, including seeking reassurance from partners or avoiding activities, negatively impacts their relationships, which can also lead to sexual issues.

Anxiety is also related to **other mental health conditions**. Just as anxiety disorders have similar underlying processes, mood disorders and anxiety disorders often overlap. As much as half the population of people with major depression also experience panic attacks. Around 95 percent of people diagnosed with depression report a current or past anxiety disorder, so GAD and major depression may occur together more often than not.

I have seen this correlation in my work, as many of my clients explain the relationship between anxiety and depression similarly. Anxiety is energizing in that it spurs us to change and control our experience. When that becomes hopeless or exhausting, resignation can set in, looking much like depression. People with depression may show different behaviors and thought patterns, but the experiential avoidance process is present. ACT, as a process-based treatment, is particularly helpful, because its methods involve changing the processes underlying suffering, and not just symptom management.

Health and Well-Being

Our bodies and minds are so tightly interwoven that what affects one part of the body affects other parts of the system. Just as chronic stress and anxiety negatively impact the body, positive physical changes can have a positive mental effect. Think about the times you were sleep deprived or went too long between meals; you might have been more irritable or anxious. When our physical health is not cared for, we are less resilient to our emotions. Improving physical health will give you more resources to handle stress and learn new skills.

Sleep

There is an abundance of research on the importance of sleep and how lack of it can harm our bodies. Learning about this can encourage people who dismiss sleep to change their behavior, but it can also cause anxiety. If you find yourself becoming anxious about sleep, using the psychological flexibility skills in this book will help you watch worries and allow your body to fall asleep in its own time. The following tips taken from research can help.

- Keep a consistent sleep routine. This helps your brain shift into "sleep mode" at the same time each day.

- Do not use your sleeping area for daytime activities. The bed and the time of day should cue our brains that sleep is imminent, and doing work or watching TV there can disrupt that behavior association. The oft-repeated advice to discontinue use of screens in bed applies here as well.

- If you are unable to sleep, you might practice mindfulness of your body as it physically rests, or complete a body scan meditation. This is not to force sleep, but to tune in to your body.

Nutrition

Our diet can have a negative impact on our bodies as well. The specific ways stress impacts the body—digestive issues, heart problems, and muscle pain—are also affected by nutrition. This is another example of how targeting one part of the system impacts the whole system.

Meals are excellent times to practice being present. When we discuss skills for being present in later chapters, you might choose to use meals as an opportunity to be present, connecting with the joy of eating and with those around you. The skills you will learn in this book to respond to your anxiety may also promote improved behaviors that promote physical health.

Pay attention to how different food affects you as well as the timing of meals. For example, for many people living with anxiety, the natural response to caffeine—including irritability, nervousness, and digestive issues—feels just like anxiety. Our minds often come to associate sensations with a story: "Oh no, there goes my chest. I must be anxious again," when this feeling is actually the natural effect of caffeine. Developing your present moment awareness will also help you notice other patterns, including how you feel when you eat breakfast, eat later in the day, or ingest a lot of sugar.

Exercise

Exercise can be incredibly helpful in managing anxiety. Exercise positively affects the very parts of our body that are negatively impacted by stress; it strengthens the heart and lungs, relieves digestive issues, and helps with sleep and muscle relaxation. The endorphins released during exercise can also lead to a sense of well-being. Finally, exercise can improve mental clarity, focus, and energy.

It is possible that exercise can be just another way to seek relief from thoughts and feelings, which is not the intent of this book. Instead, you might think of exercise as a time when your mind shifts into the present and fully experiences the moment. Find ways to joyfully move your body, whether it is taking a walk around the block at lunch or after dinner with a partner, taking up gentle yoga, or going for a swim. If you find yourself in an adversarial relationship with exercise, the flexibility skills you will learn in later chapters can help you commit to exercise without using shame, force, or avoidance.

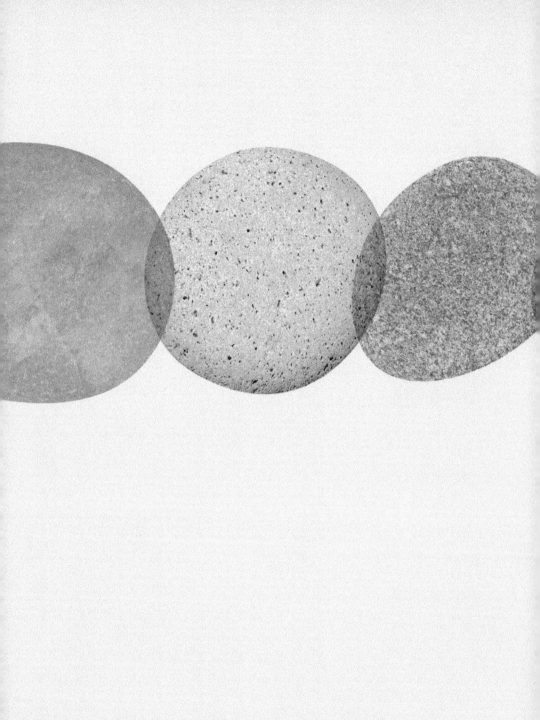

THE ACCEPTANCE AND COMMITMENT THERAPY APPROACH

ACT is more than just a therapy. It is an approach to living and learning rooted in philosophy, the rigorous study of human language, and a desire to improve the human condition. Instead of treating what is not "normal," ACT sees suffering resulting from normal processes that have become unworkable and ineffective. The goal is not to change the essential processes of the mind—a futile effort—but to change our relationship to those processes so we have more freedom to choose workable and effective actions.

This chapter contains a brief primer on ACT, including its origins and relationship to other therapies and mindfulness practices. Then we will discuss what all this means for you and your journey using ACT for anxiety. Finally, we will lay the groundwork for the skills ahead by analyzing the unworkable ways we cope with anxiety, and review core ACT concepts.

Origins of ACT

In *A Liberated Mind*, Dr. Steven C. Hayes, one of the founders of ACT, describes how his struggle with panic disorder shaped his research into human language and cognition. This research has led to a model of understanding human behavior, contextual behavioral science, which includes Relational Frame Theory (see page 26), and ACT. This foundation of philosophy, theory, and basic research allows ACT to be used for both mental health and global problems. ACT has been used for mental health conditions, including anxiety, personality disorders, and severe mental health problems; physical concerns like epilepsy, diabetes, and weight management; and global behavior change related to the Ebola pandemic and refugee crises.

ACT is part of the "third wave" of behaviorism. The first wave of behavior theory relied on research by a diverse group of scientists, including B. F. Skinner and Ivan Pavlov, who analyzed the motivations of behavior. Two processes of learned behavior identified during this time, respondent conditioning and operant conditioning, are helpful to note here.

◆ **Respondent conditioning** refers to the process of a neutral stimulus becoming associated with a stimulus that naturally evokes some reaction. An example of this is the sound of a phone's ringtone. Imagine using the same song for your incoming call alert. Before using it as a ringtone, this song may have been neutral. After a few months, however, this song will become associated with being called. If you find these phone calls unpleasant (e.g., you are called frequently by a demanding boss), you may notice yourself reacting negatively to the sound of the song, regardless of who is calling or even if you hear it on the radio. Similarly, if you enjoy getting phone calls, you might experience excitement when you hear that same sound, even when you are not being called.

- **Operant conditioning** refers to the process of increasing or decreasing the likelihood of a behavior being repeated based on reinforcement or punishment. If you are rewarded for getting to work on time with a "Nice to see you!" from someone you respect, you are more likely to arrive on time in the future. Conversely, if you come to work on time and are immediately faced with unpleasant interactions, you might be less likely to arrive on time in the future.

Cognitive behavioral therapy (CBT) is part of the second wave of behavioral theory. Many trials have shown the effectiveness of CBT, but processed-based research that investigates *how* a therapy is effective has found that the most effective part of CBT is the behavioral part. Cognitive restructuring, which attempts to replace problematic thoughts with more "rational" thoughts, shows little benefit.

Third wave behavior treatments include the use of acceptance and mindfulness. This includes dialectical behavior therapy (DBT) and ACT. ACT is unique because the theory behind it was developed first, with extensive research, before the ACT treatment was developed. In mental health, it is often the other way around.

PSYCHOLOGICAL FLEXIBILITY

ACT's goal, and by extension the goal of this book, is to increase psychological flexibility. Psychological flexibility is defined by your ability to be open to your present experience, voluntarily shifting your attention to where it is needed in the present moment, and developing habits that move your life in the direction of your most cherished values. Psychological rigidity, by contrast, is marked by our craving to escape pain by ruminating, worrying, mindlessly getting lost in activity, distracting ourselves, or stubbornly working or staying on a task, regardless of the costs to our long-term well-being. Psychological rigidity is a predictive factor in nearly all mental health problems, including anxiety. It even predicts who develops PTSD after experiencing trauma.

Fortunately, psychological flexibility can be taught, learned, and practiced. The skills that we cover in chapters 3 through 8 will help you practice psychological flexibility. Because our minds are powerful and will trap us from time to time, the practice of psychological flexibility is an ongoing life journey. Although the work is never quite "done," continued practice can bring you to flexibility faster.

ACT's Intention

Instead of viewing anxiety as a problem to be treated, ACT encourages moving toward the very source of our suffering. ACT further asserts that our tendency to try to reduce fear or anxiety is what causes suffering. Our methods of managing the dangers of the world become problems when applied to our internal world.

Imagine yourself as a young child, looking up at the stove, smelling dinner being cooked, and wondering what was up there. You reach for the stove, and . . . *ouch*! You feel the hot sensation of a burn and your hand reflexively jerks away—an expected and even helpful response. When we apply that same logic to our inner world, however, problems arise. Can you really pull away from fear, happiness, or a rapid heartbeat?

Instead of trying to suppress, control, change, or solve our internal experience, ACT gives us the alternative of learning to accept our emotions and thoughts. We then become freer to choose our behavior according to what is deeply important to us. Let's examine the components of ACT a bit more.

Acceptance

Imagine you are having a small party or get-together at your home when your housemate, Anxiety, comes in. This person is annoying. They ask if the guests are really having a good time, and wonder if you should have cooked a new dish today.

What do you want to do? One option could be to try to force Anxiety out, but they keep coming back in. Another option is to try to get away from Anxiety, but the room is small, and you cannot stay away from Anxiety for too long. You could choose to lie down in a corner, but then your guests will miss out on talking to you. Whether you are fighting, suppressing, or resigning yourself to Anxiety, you are not engaging with your guests or enjoying your party.

Acceptance is realizing that Anxiety is as a much a guest of this party as Happiness and your closest friend. You do not have to like its presence, nor do you have to make it go away, in order to connect with others, cook a meal, or have fun. In fact, you might notice that all those attempts to dodge anxiety led to more suffering than just allowing anxiety to be present. To be clear, acceptance is also not stewing in or ruminating on an emotion. Rather, it is allowing the feeling to be present while you engage in what is important to you in your life.

Commitment

I was working on acceptance with a client one day when she said, "Okay, so I accept the emotions I am feeling. Now what?" For so long, anxiety had been calling the shots: It decided how late she stayed at work, if she went to that social event on Thursday, if she was vulnerable with her wife. Now that she was accepting anxiety by allowing it to be present, she had the freedom to make decisions on her own. "Now what?" indeed!

Commitment is the process of making decisions by acting in alignment with your values. When you know what is deeply important to you, you can take steps in that direction even when anxiety shows up. Let's return to the party metaphor. If you value connecting with friends and family, sharing your home or your gift of cooking, and having fun, then you can commit to having a party that engages in all those values. If anxiety shows up, you can still cook, play a board game, and talk to your friends.

Therapy

The practice of accepting our internal experience and making choices in accordance with values, rather than our minds, is not intuitive to us. We are accustomed to problem solving, controlling, and reacting. The therapy part of ACT speaks to the process of changing behavior in pursuit of greater psychological flexibility.

ACT identifies six processes, or skills: defusion, acceptance, present moment awareness, observing self, values, and commitment. As an orientation to therapy rather than a set of skills or interventions, ACT uses therapy interventions to shift in these six areas. I will use metaphors, experiential exercises, mindfulness practices, journal entries, and more to teach and develop skills in these six areas throughout this book.

Therapy is a space to identify your own patterns, learn new behaviors, and practice those new behaviors with the encouragement of a therapist. I hope this book can be like a pocket therapist, so that you can see how these skills might affect your life, and give you an opportunity to practice them with my support along the way.

ACT Approach and Mindfulness

Mindfulness is a commonly used word these days. My favorite definition of mindfulness comes from Jon Kabat-Zinn, believed to be one of the early champions of mindfulness in the West: Mindfulness is "the awareness that arises from paying attention, on purpose, in the present moment, and non-judgmentally."

It is important to note the difference between mindfulness and meditation. Mindfulness is simply "waking up" to the present moment in the unique way Kabat-Zinn describes. Meditation is one way to practice and cultivate this awareness. Between work, family, chores, our phones, and our thoughts and emotions, our attention is constantly drawn in many different directions. Therefore, it takes practice to get control of our attention. Meditation that emphasizes controlling our attention, and not our thoughts, is one way to strengthen this ability. We can cultivate mindfulness in many other ways, however, including mindful movement like yoga, dance, or mindful walking, or the ACT skills we will cover in this book.

Mindfulness, in part because of Kabat-Zinn's work, is part of many therapy approaches. He created Mindfulness-Based Stress Reduction (MBSR) to help people struggling with chronic pain change their relationship with pain and live more full lives. MBSR gave way to Mindfulness-Based Cognitive Therapy (MBCT), which combined CBT and MBSR for people with depression.

While MBSR and MBCT explicitly draw on mindfulness for the bulk of the treatment, other modern therapies, such as DBT, include mindfulness as part of the treatment. DBT was first created to treat chronic suicidality and self-harm. The treatment is a package of skills training, individual treatment based on behavioral principles, phone coaching between sessions to improve one's use of the skills, and consultation for the therapist to ensure integrity to the model. Mindfulness is an entire module of skills in DBT and underlies much of the work. For example, group skills training sessions begin with mindfulness, and many DBT therapists practice mindfulness inside and outside of session.

ACT takes a slightly different approach to mindfulness. Although meditation can certainly be a part of successful ACT work, mindfulness meditation is not an inherent part of ACT. Instead, awareness and attention control are cultivated through skills that may last anywhere from a few seconds to several minutes. Repeatedly practicing these skills throughout the day can improve attentional control, but if you are interested in mindfulness meditation, even a few minutes a day can be effective.

RELATIONAL FRAME THEORY

Relational Frame Theory (RFT) is the theory of language that underlies ACT. Here, language is defined as the use of symbols, expressed through verbal or sign language, math, images, or even movement like dance. *Symbol*, used in this context, implies that there is nothing *inherent* in the relationship between a symbol and what it refers to. There is nothing inherent in a banana's taste, texture, sound, or appearance that makes us call it a "banana," and yet I bet some of you are seeing the fruit in your mind right now. As children, we quickly learn to relate symbols to objects (e.g., relating the sound "dog" to our actual family dog) and symbols to written representations (e.g., relating the sound "dog" to the letters D-O-G). This is the foundation for a vast and ever-growing network of relations that cannot be unlearned.

The following example shows both the arbitrary and powerful nature of symbols. The relational frame in RFT refers to our learned ability to put anything in a relationship with anything else. Let's try out this process by picking any two objects you can see in your space. When you have selected your objects, answer the following questions to yourself or in your notebook:

How is Object 1 better than Object 2? Now, how is Object 2 the opposite of Object 1?

Our minds can answer these questions even if we have never considered them before. My mind told me that a lamp is better than a book because it provides necessary light at night—perhaps to read—and a book is the opposite of a lamp because it can be put under a couch. In this example, "better than" and "opposite" are frames for the two objects selected.

Although this example may seem innocuous, there are significant implications for this process.

- First, if we can make a relationship out of anything, then trying to change our thoughts to be more rational is fruitless. There is nothing rational about making a lamp better than a book, yet my mind made that connection rapidly.

- Second, it explains how our mind can make relations even when we are not directly taught something. If I become friends with a group of people and someone tells me "John is kinder than Sarah," then someone else tells me "Sarah is kinder than Derek," my mind might conclude that Derek is unkind, even if I have no direct experience of this.

- The third important implication of relational framing is that language can and does affect our behavior. Imagine that I become cold and distant when I first meet Derek. My behavior toward him changed due to symbols instead of my direct experience of him.

Following a mental rule is not itself a problem: We regularly follow rules like "Look before stepping into the street" even though we may never have directly experienced the consequences of not doing so. Rigidly following a rule, especially when our direct experience says something different or following the rule takes us away from our values, is the problem. An example of a rigidly held rule is avoiding a movie theater although you love movies, when the rule "Don't go into cramped spaces because you can't leave if you panic" shows up.

Continued

Relational Frame Theory continued

The power of verbal relations explains why you might think of hurtful experiences from the past when someone talks about a loving relationship. This opposite frame might then lead you to become emotionally distant in a current relationship. ACT skills aim to reduce the power of symbolic thought, without trying to suppress or control this natural process. This ultimately gives you more power over your own behavior.

ACT and Anxiety

Now that you have a sense of what ACT is, you might be wondering how this approach is used to treat anxiety. Based on processes of suffering from chapter 1 (see page 4), anxiety becomes a problem when these six psychological rigidity processes occur:

◆ We are highly fused with our thoughts, by taking them literally and letting them guide our behavior.

◆ We avoid difficult feelings or thoughts.

◆ We are not present in our own lives.

◆ We have a fixed sense of ourselves.

◆ We are detached from what is truly important to us.

◆ We are distant from our goals.

ACT has a corresponding skill for each process, to ensure psychological flexibility.

Defusion will help you see thoughts for what they are: just thoughts. This reduces the power of our thoughts over our behavior. While you will still have painful thoughts and memories, and your mind will still want to worry and problem solve, defusion allows them to hold less power and allows you to freely choose your next move.

Acceptance will help you cultivate openness and willingness to experience emotions. When we become open to our internal experience, we can stop rigidly avoiding, learn from our own reactions, and better move toward what is important.

Presence will teach you to have more attentional control. When your mind is not jumping to the past or planning for the future, you can pay attention to the present moment in a helpful way. This might be experiencing the joy of being with people you love without planning for catastrophe, or even being able to connect with someone new without rigidly checking to see if you are anxious.

Viewing your experience from the perspective of **the observing self** will allow you to witness the present moment nonjudgmentally, see yourself as a complete person, and connect with the perspective of others. It also allows us to take other perspectives, which increases empathy and our ability to receive feedback from others without defense.

The preceding skills will allow you to get in touch with your deepest **values**. When we are no longer at the mercy of rules and expectations, space opens up to allow us to make free choices. These choices may range from how we want to spend either this Saturday or the next 10 years. Either way, values will help you figure out how you want to spend your time and take action.

Finally, when you have a strong foundation of skills and you know where to go, the only thing left to do is take **committed action**. This is where ACT becomes fluid and responsive to what is happening for you in the present. As we move toward our values, fear surfaces, our old stories show up, and our mind begs us to go to the safety of numbness and avoidance. The ACT skills will prepare you to compassionately unhook from these thoughts and continue to move forward. We all inevitably move away from our values. All six parts of ACT will help you notice when you have moved away from your values and move toward them again.

Problem Solving in Overdrive

MATERIALS: Journal
SUGGESTED TIME: 5 minutes

Before we jump into the ACT skills, it's important to identify ways you are already avoiding, suppressing, or controlling your internal experience. Without this awareness, many people inadvertently use ACT skills to continue controlling their thoughts and emotions. For example, you may think, "Okay, I am nervous about my presentation. If I stay nervous, it won't go well. I'll try some mindfulness techniques to calm down. Am I calm yet? No, there is anxiety. Why isn't this working?"

We are going to work to change your relationship with your mind, which takes a lot of practice. For that to be successful, we must carefully observe the ways our mind wants to take control.

First, let's get into contact with the helpful part of your problem-solving mind.

- Imagine that the power goes out as you are reading this. Take a few moments now to consider your options and what you might do next. You might write some down in your journal.

- Notice how these options might help you, and how quickly your ideas came to mind.

- My mind identified the following options: waiting a few minutes to see if power returns, digging out a flashlight, using my phone to search for known outages, and going outside to see how far the blackout goes. Look at all those ideas generated in just a few moments! You might have come up with even more or different options. This is our problem-solving mind at its best.

Now let's get in contact with the unhelpful aspects of your problem-solving mind.

- Consider a psychological problem you have been experiencing—perhaps difficult memories, panic attacks, or constant worry about the future. Clearly define the problem in your mind and write it in your journal.

- Next, consider all the ways you have tried to solve that problem. Consider how you distract yourself, the ways you avoid the concern, and the ways thoughts function to problem solve.

- Finally, identify the problem-solving behaviors that have worked over the long-term.

As an example, here are Blair's answers:

- I am struggling to finish my thesis project for my degree. I feel panic every time I think about it.

- How I distract myself: I exercise, research a new computer, work more on other projects, watch TV, eat, read books.

- How I avoid: I don't check my email in case my thesis advisor has emailed me. I sleep and nap.

- How I use thoughts to problem solve: I worry about failing or taking an incomplete to get more time; I wonder what would have happened if I did not go back to school; I consider dropping out; I make to-do lists.

- What has worked: None of these. I feel better in the short-term, sometimes for the rest of the day. In the end, though, my thesis is not done and I really want to graduate.

You will notice that Blair's list includes many behaviors that seem "good" or "healthy," but context matters! Reading, exercising, or sleeping to avoid anxiety become a problem if they take you away from your work, your family, or your relationships.

Glossary of ACT Terms

ACCEPTANCE: The act of being open and willing to experience an emotion, sensation, or thought

ACT PROCESS: The steps, techniques, or skills used to shift our relationship with our mind, thus reducing the power that internal experiences, including anxiety, have on our behavior. The six processes are defusion, acceptance, present moment awareness, observing self, identifying values, and committed action.

BEHAVIOR: Any actions by a whole organism in and within a context; for humans, this includes overt actions as well as thoughts, emotions, sensations, memories

COMMITTED ACTION: Actions in line with values that lead to larger patterns of action over time

CONCEPTUALIZED SELF: The opposite of observing self; fusion with stories about the self and lacking flexible perspective

DEFUSION: The act of taking thoughts less literally, thus reducing the power they have; for example, hearing *banana* as a series of sounds instead of imagining the fruit

EXPERIENTIAL AVOIDANCE: Efforts to change, control, or suppress experience; distraction, opting out of events, worrying, saying "I'm okay," working, exercising, and more can all function as experiential avoidance if the intent is to control emotions or thoughts; experiential avoidance can occur with any emotion, including happiness

FUNCTIONAL CONTEXTUALISM: The philosophy at the root of ACT; it is pragmatic, defining "truth" as "what works"

FUSION: Taking thoughts as literal truth, which allows them to influence behavior without conscious awareness; we are often fused to rules without even consciously knowing that we are (see: Rules)

LANGUAGE: The ability to use symbols and create relationships between symbols

MINDFULNESS: Flexible, nonjudgmental attention in the present moment

OBSERVING SELF: The act of perceiving yourself in a given context, rather than as a fixed self; this is also known as self-as-context

PSYCHOLOGICAL FLEXIBILITY: The ability to be open to thoughts and emotions and flexibly move your attention to take actions that are consistent with what you identify as important

RELATIONAL FRAME: Refers to the learned process of putting stimuli (objects, situations, people, behaviors) in relation to each other

RULES: A relationship between a behavior and expected consequences, often without direct experience; examples include "I have to control my emotions to be effective," or "Having a panic attack means I am crazy"; rules are neither good nor bad (suffering occurs when we rigidly obey a rule despite our values or lived experience)

SYMBOL: Something that stands for something else, in an arbitrary way, meaning that it does not reflect the object's characteristics or inherent qualities

VALUES: Qualities of being and living that are deeply important to you; values are freely chosen and are not rules

WORKABILITY: The degree to which a behavior moves us closer to our goals and values; the guiding litmus test in ACT, rather than the "truth" of a thought, emotion, or action

3

COGNITIVE DEFUSION

t is hard to make lasting changes when our minds dictate our every move. If you are trying to conquer anxiety and engage fully in life by creating new relationships, being assertive at work, or returning to school to obtain a degree, your mind will show up and tell you the terrible things that could happen and how the old path is safer. "Better stick to what you know," it might say. So before we take steps to live a bold, full life, we need skills to use when our minds try to steer us away from our true desires. The first process we will discuss is defusion.

In this chapter, you will learn what defusion is, and how it will help you with anxiety. You will learn defusion techniques, and how to successfully use them to create distance from thoughts. The examples will help illustrate the process and the benefits of defusion, and prepare you to incorporate it into your everyday life. Finally, there will be a series of exercises to try.

Behind the Method

If you recall the section on RFT in chapter 2, when I learned that John was kinder than Sarah and that Sarah was kinder than Derek, my mind concluded that Derek was the least kind of all of them. That rapid, automatic ability to form a relationship between two things without prior experience is innately human.

Thinking "Derek is unkind" is not itself a problem. Following the rule "If I am vulnerable with someone who has hurt me in the past, then I will get hurt again" is not inherently a problem, either. Problems arise from rigidly following these thoughts and rules, especially if they go against our values or contradict lived experience.

Notice that the thought "Derek is unkind" is not a literal experience of knowing Derek, nor is the rule "If I am vulnerable with someone who has hurt me in the past, then I will get hurt again." Imagine that I do spend some time with Derek. If I am highly fused to these thoughts, I might interpret his sense of humor as mocking. I might be cold or standoffish. This behavior leads me away from my values of warmth, connection, and generosity, and prevents me from getting to know the real Derek.

If I defused from the thoughts "Derek is unkind" and "I can't open up to him because I will get hurt," I might be more present with his behavior, noticing his dry sense of humor and his quiet politeness. Being more open, I might share something appropriately vulnerable with him, and observe how he responds. Maybe I will still decide to have a more distant relationship anyway, but I will reach this decision through direct experience and values, not thoughts. If he responds supportively, I could develop a friendship with someone I would not have if I had remained fused.

Anything that causes you to view your thoughts as thoughts, instead of a literal experience of the world, is defusion. Defusion means looking *at* our thoughts, rather than *from* our thoughts. You will get plenty of ideas and exercises in this chapter, but also know that you can get creative. ACT is all about workability, which is defined as anything moving you closer to your values. If what you are doing moves you closer to viewing your thoughts as simply thoughts, then that is likely defusion.

Many of the exercises in this chapter rely on taking the literal content out of thoughts. We can often get wrapped up in the content of the thought: if it's true or false, if it's crazy, or what it means for our future. We can take a step back from our thoughts instead.

One sign of defusion is having a kind sense of humor about your thoughts. When I can have a little chuckle at a thought, I know I am defused from it. This humor is not a mean-spirited mocking, but a knowing laugh at the messiness of our minds.

Another indicator is increased flexibility. This might appear as literally opening up in the body—a feeling of lightness or space— or a feeling of having more options available to you. The goal of defusion is opening up to our world to give us more information and options.

DEFUSION VERSUS FUSION

If defusing is like waking up from a dream, being fused is like being in the dream; it is hard to tell you are in it, but once you notice where you are, it changes everything. Here are some examples of fusion:

- **Mental "ping-ponging," or what I call "the courtroom drama."** Your mind divides over multiple options and argues it out. This might happen when deciding what to have for lunch or if you should take a new job.

- **Feeling indecisive or "stuck."** This can lead to avoidance or distraction as you wait for your mind to make itself up. (Spoiler alert: it won't.)

- **Repetitive thoughts.** This is most clear when you are talking out your thoughts and notice you have already made a certain point.

- **Perfectionism or obsessively staying on a task past its work-ability.** This might mean fusion with a rule about how things need to look before being considered finished or a rule about productivity.

- **Avoidance and distraction.** Any of the behaviors that you listed in the Problem Solving in Overdrive exercise (see page 32) likely indicate that fusion is present.

While not an exhaustive list, all these are indicators that it is time for defusion.

Continued

Defusion is the waking up from the dream. You still have thoughts, but they do not hold the same urgency they had just a second ago. You might notice feeling more open, or a sense of direction. This sometimes feels like an internal calmness even if you are in a stressful situation, but remember that we are not seeking a specific internal state. A sense of clarity of purpose, humor, and compassion often accompany defusion. If you are beating yourself up for thoughts, you are not defused—at least not from self-critical thoughts!

Defusion Techniques

Knowing defusion techniques is one thing, but the ability to apply them is another. I will repeat this often: Practice each skill frequently. The first few times you practice a new skill will help you learn how it works and get it in your mind as an option. Then, you will begin to apply the ones that resonate with you.

Below are metaphors and techniques that I and other ACT therapists have used to teach defusion. I have also included how these skills have worked with others. These techniques are helpful when first learning defusion, and any time you need to defuse from a sticky thought. Use the indicators in the previous sidebar as guides for when to use any of these exercises. Try them all a few times before finding your favorites.

Sing Your Thoughts

This is a classic ACT skill. At the heart of singing your thoughts is allowing them not to be so literal. This exercise can be helpful with especially "sticky" thoughts that your mind is determined to keep around. Find an easy melody to sing along to, such as "Happy Birthday," and replace your thought with the original lyrics of the song.

Name Your Mind

This is one of my favorite defusion exercises. Come up with a name for your mind. I recommend that this name not be relationally connected to any provocative content, such as a name of a parent or old relationship. When I named my mind Monica, the name came quite quickly and, to date, I do not have any significant associations with the name Monica. Now each time my mind gets really active and opinionated, I say, "Oh hi, Monica, didn't see you there." Instead of engaging in her content, I might think, "Thanks, Monica, I've got it from here." If she says something particularly cruel, I might say

"Okay, Monica, I appreciate your input." Thanking your mind in an authentic way is an excellent way to change your relationship to it.

My Mind Is Having the Thought That . . .

This prompt is great to give you a little space from your mind. You might have to try it a few thoughts in a row to start noticing its effect. If you have a difficult thought that takes a lot of power from you, simply restate it with *"My mind is having the thought that . . ."* before the content of your thought.

For example, when Sam meets someone new, she thinks, "This person is going to take advantage of me." When she is fused with this thought, she experiences anxiety, and her mind jumps into problem solving and worrying. When she practices this technique, she says, "My mind is having the thought that this person is going to take advantage of me." She does this for any follow-up thoughts. For example, she might say, "My mind is having the thought that I should stay vigilant," and/or "My mind is having the thought that this technique won't work." This is not about finding the right or true thought, but instead just noticing that thoughts are the creation of our minds.

Where Does This Thought Take Me?

This technique takes a pragmatic approach to thoughts. Noticing how the thought will affect your behavior gives you the choice to follow the thought or not. For example, Sam had the thought that she would have a panic attack if she went to an upcoming meeting, and that a panic attack would mortify her. She asked herself, "If I follow this thought, where does it take me?" She knew from experience that if she listened to the thought "Going to the meeting will lead to a panic attack and that would be a disaster," then one of the following would occur:

◆ She would go to the meeting but do breathing exercises the whole time. She knew these breathing exercises stopped her from being present and made her obsessive about her breathing. Also recall from chapter 1 that breathing exercises can worsen a panic disorder (see page 7).

- ◆ She would go to the meeting, but leave immediately if she became anxious.
- ◆ She would just skip the meeting.

Sam realized that following this thought actually took her away from her values to be present and engaged at work. The thought was unhelpful, so she decided to attend the meeting anyway and use acceptance skills discussed later in this chapter (see page 48).

Name That Story!

For this technique, name or label a frequent thought process as if you are naming a film. For example, if your mind regularly worries about appearing awkward to others, you might name the thought *The I Am So Awkward Story*. Or if your mind worries about things going wrong, you can say, "There's the *Everything is Falling Apart Story* again." Shorter labels can also be helpful. We all have an inner critic that criticizes us and the world around us. You might label this thought process *The Judge*. If you find yourself frequently problem-solving your emotions, that's *The Problem Solver*. If you get lost in explaining the intentions of others or having debates in your mind that never occur, you're observing *The Storyteller*. The goal is to step out of the process and see it for the fusion that it is.

Jordan's Experience with Defusion

Jordan was fused with many judgments about himself, along with rules about how to be in relationships. To start, we discussed naming his mind. Jordan worried at first that it would make him look "crazy" if he referred to his mind in the third person. I asked him if he would be willing to proceed with the skill even if his mind threw "You're crazy" at him, and he agreed.

Our minds love to think, plan, and problem solve, and will often rebel at our attempts to defuse. Let's consider fusion like a dance. Your mind is a professional dancer who knows all the best moves, and throws a thought at you to rile you up, starting the routine. For you, this dance is merely exhausting. When we decline our mind's invitation to dance, it often throws more material at us to get us dancing again.

Jordan named his mind, then tried one of the defusion exercises, Ducks on a Pond (see page 53). He returned to tell me that he had a difficult interaction with his dad that triggered many of his "You're a bad son" thoughts. After a few minutes in this shame spiral, he decided to name his mind, then practiced Ducks on a Pond. He said that after he finished the exercises, he felt resentment and sadness about his relationship with his father. We noticed that "You're a bad son" prevented him from holding the very vulnerable emotions of resentment and sadness. It was as if his mind preferred shame, even though it had made him suffer for years. Shortly after this, his mind began the judging "You're bad" story again. This is normal; we sometimes need to practice defusion over and over again.

While not every defusion exercise works for everyone, it is worth trying each a few times, even if your mind protests, to see what your experience is telling you. While Jordan would not always defuse from this story, after identifying its purpose and practicing defusion, he could get more and more distance from it. Once he defused regularly, we were able to move on to acceptance skills for his painful emotions.

Misconceptions

Defusion is not arguing with or suppressing thoughts. Defusion is not saying, "Derek is kind and I am going to open up to him." It is not adding more thoughts to suppress thoughts like, "You're so judgmental; give Derek a chance." It is simply noticing the thought as a thought.

Defusion is also not trying to feel a certain way. Earlier in this chapter, we discussed various signs of defusion. It is important to recognize that we do not engage in these skills to feel or experience different emotions or sensations. The only goal of defusion is to make thoughts less literal and less powerful over our behavior. Defusion can open up difficult emotions, like it did for Jordan. As he defused from the "You're a terrible son" story, he made room for resentment and hurt. The self-critical thoughts served to avoid the painful emotions.

Sometimes defusion allows people to fully be present with a painful past or trauma. Acceptance skills, discussed in the next chapter, will be particularly helpful if that occurs for you. For now, know that if those feelings show up, it is not a sign of failed defusion. In fact, it signals that you have started to change your relationship with your mind, allowing yourself to feel new emotions and experiences.

The following exercises will help you deepen your ability to defuse from difficult thoughts. The first two exercises can help you change your relationship to a thought quickly as you go about your day. The third exercise is more meditative and can help you become observant if you are having racing thoughts.

Cookie, Cookie, Cookie

MATERIALS: Timer or clock with a second hand
SUGGESTED TIME: 1 to 2 minutes

Thoughts are "sticky" when we take them literally, as if they paint a completely accurate portrait of the world. One way to defuse from the power of words is to think of thoughts as symbols, sounds we utter to make meaning. This exercise will help you do this.

1. Imagine a cookie: the sweet smell, the taste, the texture in your mouth. Notice that even when an actual cookie is not present, we can contact the sensations associated with one. You might even notice salivation or your stomach rumbling, all because of a thought.

2. When you are ready, set your clock for 30 seconds, and repeat "cookie" to yourself for the whole time.

3. What did you notice? Every time I complete this exercise, I notice how the sound of the word "cookie" feels in my throat and on my tongue. It also starts to sound like "kooky," then a series of the "k" sound.

4. Now, you will repeat this exercise with a painful thought, maybe a judgment about yourself. For example, you might have the thought "I'm not good enough. I'm just such a failure." If you get hooked on that thought, it can turn into a spiral of thoughts listing all your disappointments. Alternatively, you might get caught in a courtroom drama, with one side listing evidence of your failures and the other side listing achievements. You are hooked either way, and this thought has the power to make your next decisions.

5. Identify a word that sums up a judgment about yourself. If you are struggling to identify one, the word "failure" often provokes emotions.

6. Set your timer for 30 seconds, and repeat the word you choose for 30 seconds.

7. If you find yourself stumbling over the word, laughing at its sound, or noticing tension leaving your shoulders, you are probably becoming defused. Now you have more freedom to make a different decision. If this thought came up because you made a mistake, you might be able to clear-headedly problem solve it. If it came up during an argument with a partner, you might be able to clearly talk to them about their feelings, while staying true to your values.

8. Practice this exercise every time your mind gets fused to a thought. It will help you defuse, so you can freely choose your next behavior.

Try this exercise daily so that you can see how it works for you in different scenarios. Daily practice means you will be flexibly trying defusion every day, several times a day, which makes it easier to continue with the skills ahead.

Passengers on the Bus

MATERIALS: Journal
SUGGESTED TIME: Varies

"Passengers on the Bus" is a frequently used metaphor adapted from the original founders of ACT. Because this metaphor has all six ACT processes within it, we will return to it throughout the book. For this exercise, we will use it for defusion. I will introduce the metaphor below, and then follow up with instructions on how to use it for defusion.

Think of life like driving a bus. You are the bus driver, deciding where to go. You pick up passengers along the way that represent thoughts, emotions, memories, and sensations. Sometimes these passengers are helpful, like when they tell you someone is about to walk across the street. Other times they are controlling and demanding, and instruct you to take a different route.

Here are examples of how passengers—or thoughts—can get people stuck:

◆ When you are about to take action, like ask for a promotion or go on a date, a passenger tells you to go home instead, and you do.

◆ To silence your passengers, you appease them by following their demands, and trick yourself over time into thinking that is what you want (e.g., "I don't like going out anyway").

◆ You might stop and demand that the passengers leave. However, they do not leave, and every second you fight with them is a second you are not moving where you want to go.

What if you went where you wanted to go, even when passengers showed up? That is the goal of this exercise. An example follows to help you see the exercise in action.

- To start, identify an area where you are struggling, perhaps an area you are avoiding, or a fearful situation. Close your eyes and imagine yourself in this area of your life. Notice the thoughts that come up. Collect as many details as you can.

- Write the area of your life that you have identified in your journal, and write the thoughts that came to mind underneath.

- Now let's name those passengers. Close your eyes again, and imagine one of those thoughts. What might this thought look like if it were a person? You might think of someone you know or a stranger. Does this passenger have a name?

- Be careful not to create an adversarial relationship with your passengers. We are not trying to stop or eliminate passengers here.

- Notice what this passenger is *trying* to do. Are they trying to protect you? Are they trying to help you improve?

- What happens when you listen to this passenger? Is that workable?

- Note what you learn in your journal.

- Repeat this process for the other thoughts.

- To apply this in your life, you can use a technique similar to Name Your Mind (see page 43). When you notice this particular passenger, you can gently label them in your mind by saying "Oh, there is [Passenger Name]."

As an example, Claire completed this exercise. Here are her notes:

- AREA: Completing my work at the end of the day and also feeling the urge to relax.

- THOUGHTS: I just want to relax. I'm too stressed to finish it. If I don't finish it, my boss will be unhappy. I'm going to get fired.

- PASSENGERS: I named the first two thoughts "Ben." He appeared relaxed and quiet to me. This passenger seems to want to look out for my comfort and self-care, but when I listen to him, I behave self-indulgently. The other thoughts are "Nancy." She was dressed in a business suit and was very stern. Nancy looks out for my career and what is important to me in that domain, but does so in a mean and critical way.

- I will label the thoughts around relaxing and taking time off as "Ben" and the thoughts of working hard as "Nancy" to defuse from both. I will then let my values guide my behavior, instead of my passengers.

Ducks on a Pond

MATERIALS: Timer or clock with a second hand
SUGGESTED TIME: 3 to 5 minutes

This is a variation of a classic ACT exercise, Leaves on a Stream. I find this exercise most helpful when a mind is racing, indecisive, or adversarial. Read through the prompt, then try it on your own. You can also ask a friend to record themselves reading the exercise, with pauses between lines.

1. Set your timer for 3 to 5 minutes, depending on how much time you have or how sticky the thoughts are.

2. Find a comfortable position that you can sustain for a few minutes. Imagine yourself sitting on the banks of a large pond, with ducks swimming lazily from one side to the other. If visualizations are difficult for you, you can also imagine ducks on a simple conveyor belt or a blank space.

3. Once you have your image, place each thought you have on a duck, and let it drift by.

4. Notice if you are hurrying a duck along that has a painful thought, or keeping a duck around that has a pleasant thought. Allow your thoughts to move at their own pace instead.

5. Place thoughts that are words, as well as thoughts that are images, on the ducks.

6. If a sensation grabs your attention, put it into words and place them on a duck. For example, "There's anxiety," or "There's restlessness."

7. You will inevitably get stuck to a thought again, finding yourself more with the ducks in the water than on the side of the

Continued

pond. This is perfectly natural. Once you notice this, place your attention back on the banks of the pond, and begin placing thoughts on the ducks again.

8. Sometimes thoughts return or stay in a loop. You can keep putting the thought on a different duck each time. You might also notice that some ducks will swim in a circle in front of you before moving on; allow the ducks to go at their own pace.

9. When you are ready to return to your day, more defused from thoughts, let go of this image and return to the room.

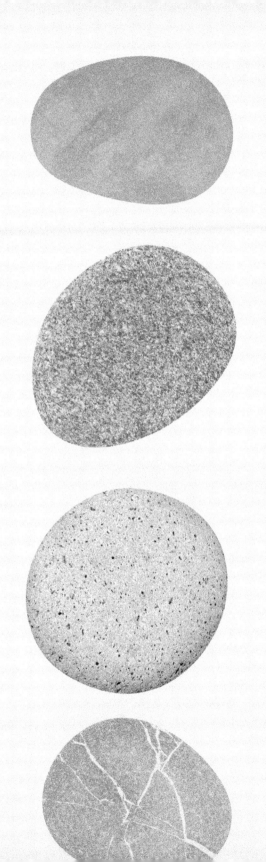

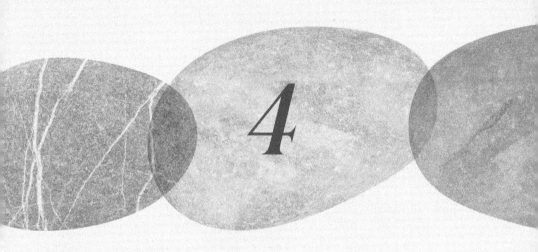

4

ACCEPTANCE

Acceptance plays a significant role in the psychological flexibility that we will cultivate through ACT. Broadly speaking, acceptance is opening up to your experience. This definition includes defusion, presence, and self-as-context skills, in addition to specific acceptance skills we will cover in this chapter. These acceptance skills are targeted to emotions and sensations because these experiences are what we avoid, control, or suppress when we engage in experiential avoidance.

When fear or anxiety show up, physical sensations also surface. Our minds often tell us that these sensations are unbearable and must be solved. However, the cycle of feeling fear, trying to control it, then worrying about the next experience of anxiety is a core process of disordered anxiety. When we go against our minds and open to our sensations and emotions, we often find there is space for the feeling. There we find freedom to pursue our goals and dreams.

In this chapter, I will review acceptance, cover a few introductory skills and misconceptions, and include a few exercises for you to incorporate acceptance into your life. Daily practice of an acceptance skill will assist you in adapting it into your life.

Behind the Method

Defusion often creates space for emotions and sensations to come up. Remember that the process behind GAD and other anxiety disorders involves the use of worry, or abstract thought, to avoid, problem-solve, and suppress more emotionally charged thoughts. So, it makes sense that when we defuse from problem solving and verbal content, then tender, painful material shows up. That is where acceptance comes in.

Acceptance in ACT is defined as willingly experiencing the vast array of human emotions *in pursuit of what is important* to us. It is the opposite of experiential avoidance. I will also use the word "willingness" as a synonym for acceptance. Willingness is taking action with an openness to whatever emotions or sensations arise.

I focus on the idea that we practice acceptance in pursuit of a valued life, to differentiate acceptance from seeking out needless pain. I would not ask anyone to see a gory slasher film to practice acceptance, for example, if that is not something they value. However, if you told me that the horror genre is really important to you, but you avoid it now because your mind has intrusive worries that you might become violent (a common experience for people with OCD), then watching a horror movie would be the perfect acceptance exercise for you.

I often hear acceptance used in the context of accepting external events: "My partner left me. I just have to accept that." "They need to accept their chronic illness." So, why focus so much on accepting internal experiences?

◆ First, many events are inherently neutral; our minds and their attachments to stories and plans decide if an event is acceptable or not. Often, we anticipate the consequences of the present moment, like when we are stuck in traffic and imagine our boss being upset at our tardiness. Even with chronic pain, stories like "I can't live with this pain another second" or "This is unbearable" serve to worsen the pain.

- Second, our normal response to losing a relationship or receiving a chronic diagnosis is grief and sadness. These are normal and valid responses. However, if our mind does not allow that response, or tries to control future losses through worry and vigilance, then we are not fully accepting our grief and the humanity within it. When we become open to the full human experience, we leave room to grieve, which allows us to more fully accept the ups and downs of living a full life.

- Finally, because of relational frames, emotions like happiness and joy can become linked to sadness, fear, and anger. Our hope can remind us of what we can lose. Our happiness can remind us of our sadness. Eventually even happiness, hope, or joy can become distressing. This leads to a life of numbness.

About 30 minutes into the "Healing from Within" episode of Bill Moyers's 1993 PBS documentary series, *Healing and the Mind* (freely available online; see References, page 148), we see MBSR founder Jon Kabat-Zinn leading a class of people who have chronic pain. Dan, who has three separate fractures in his back, is one of the participants. Dan talks about how the nerve pain has taken away his job as a carpenter, daily tasks with his wife, and even bonding fully with his son. In class, Jon invites him up and says, "I'm your pain. What do you want to tell me?" Dan playfully pushes Jon and replies, "I don't want you anymore!" to which Jon says, "But I'm here! Here I am. So, what can be done?" Jon adds, "I'm not going away. You can live around the corners of me and develop your life in some way around me."

This scene beautifully captures acceptance. The pain of being human and experiencing the uncertainty of the future, the certainty of loss, the fragility of life, and our own mortality is not going away. Through acceptance, we can live around it, creating a life amongst the pain. Acceptance asks all of us, "Are you willing to experience this to have a full life?"

Anything that you are resisting in an unworkable way, or a way that does not bring you toward your values, needs to be accepted. In chapter 1, I shared Sasha's story (see page 4). To resist the fear of eviction from her apartment, her mind worried and attempted to problem solve. What she needed to accept in that moment were sensations like her heart dropping, her stomach tensing, and her throat closing when her mind created an image of her coming home to an eviction notice. When she learned to open up to sensations like these, she was able to come to the present moment—where she was not in trouble—and continue with her day without losing energy or time planning for a future that did not exist.

ACCEPTANCE
IN THE ACT CONTEXT

When an infant or animal experiences extreme, acute pain, they cry out. The sound of their cry often alerts someone to help them. Once we develop the capacity for symbolic language, we develop new ways to experience pain. For me and many of my clients, there is something fascinating about physically recognizing the sensations of fear or sadness or guilt. When we sit with those sensations fully, we often recognize that they are uncomfortable, but not at the level of pain that would prompt an animal or infant to cry out. Our minds create stories that lead us to believe that these sensations are unbearable.

Let me share an example. In chapter 1, I introduced Charlie, who had a fear of traveling outside the radius of his work and home, because he feared having a panic attack (see page 9). He described sitting in his car, pulled over on the side of the road, with his heart racing and his breathing labored. His mind would yell, "This is terrible. I can't do this. I need to go home right now. This is unbearable." It was a moment of real suffering for Charlie. In a moment, however, he was able to observe this mental chatter, witness the suffering, and realize that he needed to practice an acceptance skill. That moment of observation included defusion, observing self, and presence—a great example of how all the ACT skills work together. Charlie then explored the sensations he was experiencing. He watched his heart beat quickly. When his mind chimed in with another thought, he brought his attention back to his chest. He noticed that the sensation was uncomfortable, but that it was not painful, and certainly not unbearable. As he watched this,

his heartbeat slowed to a more normal rhythm. This did not happen because he was trying to suppress the emotion, but as the emotion naturally ebbed and flowed.

So much of Charlie's suffering was the result of his mind. Once he opened up space for the sensations of fear outside of his mind's interpretations and stories, he found more power to tolerate and accept the fullness of his experience. He was able to start his car again and calmly go where he needed to go.

Acceptance Techniques

The following techniques include metaphors and ways to incorporate acceptance into your life. Acceptance is a relationship to our own experience, not a finalized state of being. These techniques will allow you to shift toward, rather than away from, your experience.

Drop the Rope

The physical aspect of this metaphor is powerful, so I encourage you to ask someone close to you to act out this exercise with you. Simply hold one end of a rope, towel, or belt, and have a friend or loved one hold the other end. Then, imagine you are on one side of a giant pit. Your anxiety is on the other side, and both of you are holding onto a rope. When anxiety pulls the rope, you fear falling into the pit, so you pull back. When you pull the rope, anxiety pulls back. This tug-of-war has been going on for years.

If you are doing this with someone, notice the energy it takes to stay in this tug-of-war. Are you able to focus on playing, laughing, or loving someone?

What are your options? As the name suggests, you can drop the rope, stay out of the pit, and stop fighting anxiety. Moving forward, notice what it feels like when you metaphorically pick up the rope to fight with your experience. See what it would be like in those moments to drop the rope and sit with your present experience.

Ride the Wave

This one is particularly useful for urges or sensations that lead to unworkable behavior. When you notice a strong urge to perform an action that is not serving you, watch that urge as if it is a wave. Sometimes, it will hit you harder, then recede, then return again. Follow the sensation as it rises, then falls. Be careful not to get caught up in mental stories here, such as "I have to do that action. The urge is too powerful." The mind often keeps a wave at its peak longer by storytelling.

Self-Compassion Break

This technique is adapted from Dr. Kristin Neff's research on self-compassion. While this exercise does not come from an ACT researcher, it is still consistent with how ACT describes acceptance. When you are distressed, take a moment to pause and breathe. Put your hand over your heart and say to yourself, "This is suffering. This is a moment of stress." Connect with that pain for a moment. Then say to yourself, "I'm not alone." Connect with the pain of being human. Finally, put your hand over your heart and ask yourself how you can be kind to yourself. Ask how you can accept your emotions as they are.

Saying Yes

Acceptance is like saying yes to life. Consider a situation that you are struggling with. When you encounter that situation and mentally say no to it and resist it, how does your body react? When I have asked others to practice saying no to a situation for a minute, they notice that they are turned inward, arms crossed, head down, brow furrowed. They are not open or receptive to the world.

On the other hand, imagine saying yes to this situation, practicing a willingness to experience it. How might your body act then? Others have described that their shoulders are back, their palms open, their face softens. They are open to life.

You're Not the Boss of Me!

Practice going against what your mind says in a playful way. This is not a forceful technique. If your mind is a bit like a bossy parent, you can cheerfully choose your own path. When your mind tells you to avoid the stairs because it might raise your heart rate, take the stairs anyway. When your mind instructs you not to return an email or make a phone call, immediately do the opposite, just because. Take these actions with a playful, compassionate energy.

Mae's Experience with Acceptance

Anxiety showed up in Mae's life every day. She worried about pleasing her coworkers, about her partner's emotions and feelings, about her own happiness and needs, and about getting hurt if she changed anything in her life. She also worried about being "too much" for everyone around, often feeling all these emotions at once, and suppressing them so no one knew.

One day, she came into our session in a panic. Her mind was quickly cycling through every action she had taken that day and coming up with reasons why they were failures. Her mind was telling her that she was a terrible partner and lazy employee. She was near tears. I mentioned that her mind was really beating her up with the failure stick, and this metaphor allowed her to take a tiny step back from the content of her thoughts. We did a version of the acceptance meditation together that I lay out in the exercise section below. I prompted Mae to return to her sensations of fear instead of getting caught up in thinking and judging. I asked her to observe the sensation. She would later say it was like an animal frantically running back in forth in her chest. When I asked her to hold this sensation in her hand, tears slipped out of her eyes. When I asked if we could continue, she nodded silently.

This is willingness and acceptance. It is observing pain, even when it makes us sad, and saying, "Yes, I want to continue."

After this first exercise, Mae continued to practice openness to emotions. She changed jobs, changed the nature of her relationship to make it more authentic to her identity, and started telling people how she felt. She could give me feedback on our relationship, and we could have a vulnerable and honest conversation about treatment because of her willingness to be with any emotion that showed up.

Misconceptions

You might remember my unwelcome party crasher, Anxiety, from chapter 2 (see page 22). I love this metaphor because it clearly points out what acceptance is not. Acceptance is not resignation. It is not lying on the floor, giving up, and letting your mind spin terrible tales of woe. Rather, it is experiencing your present in the present, which means also defusing from your mind's stories. Acceptance also does not mean "marinating" in your pain. I use this term playfully to capture that moment that many of us have experienced when we tell our minds, "Fine! You win! Let's be anxious!"

"Marinating" is similar to holding onto emotion, as if Anxiety tries to leave your party and you pull them back in, saying "You wanted to be here, and now you've got to stay." True acceptance is accepting our experience as it is. If anxiety is present, it is accepting of that. If anxiety leaves and contentedness ensues, it is accepting of that, as well.

Acceptance is not condoning, forgetting, or continuing the unworkable behavior of others, either. Shane (who uses they/them pronouns) was in a relationship with their girlfriend, who often yelled at Shane, blamed them for her emotions, and made demands of them. This prompted a lot of anxiety for Shane. A self-proclaimed "worrier" before, they began experiencing panic attacks and digestive issues because of how frequently their mind tried to problem solve someone else's behavior, emotions, and thoughts. Shane was often exhausted by this pattern with their girlfriend. When we covered acceptance, we discussed how they could accept the helplessness they felt in their relationship. Shane could drop the rope of trying to "fix" their girlfriend's emotions. They decided they would not accept the treatment they received in their relationship. Through accepting the helplessness, Shane learned to make requests and set boundaries. Eventually, Shane followed their values by ending the relationship as compassionately as they could.

Finally, acceptance is not rigid. Acceptance does not look like sitting with every thought, emotion, sensation, or urge that crosses your mind. It means opening up, in pursuit of your values, to what you have been avoiding.

The following exercises will help you experience acceptance. The first is a meditative exercise to practice acceptance of difficult emotions. The second exercise will help you practice willingness to experience sensations and emotions in pursuit of values. The third exercise will continue our use of the Passengers on the Bus metaphor (see page 50) to practice acceptance of difficult internal states.

Acceptance Meditation

MATERIALS: Timer
SUGGESTED TIME: 5 to 10 minutes

This exercise is done seated for 5 to 10 minutes, or as long as it takes for you to have an accepting attitude toward your emotions. You may choose to practice this meditative exercise a portion at a time, or ask someone close to you to record themselves reading it slowly so you can play it back.

There might not be an intense emotion present the first time you practice this exercise. In that case, call to mind a situation that prompts moderately intense emotions or urges. This can be something like a memory that prompts distress, imagining yourself in a feared situation, or even picturing going out to buy a box of cookies to eat after dinner.

1. Sit with your eyes closed or gazing unfocused at the floor. Without changing your breath, turn your attention to your breathing. Notice sensations as you breathe.

2. Turn your attention to the part of your body that holds this emotion. If you are unsure, take a moment to briefly scan from your head to your toes. Many emotions are felt in the middle portion of our bodies: throats, shoulders, chest, stomach, abdomen. Scan through this area until you can locate a sensation related to this emotion.

3. Observe this sensation as if you are an anthropologist watching a town square. Notice the comings and goings of sensations in a dispassionate, curious way.

Continued

4. Notice if the sensation moves, changes, or shifts. If it does not, that's okay. If it does, that's okay. Either way, do not try to change the sensation.

5. Next, find the edges of the sensation. Where does it start and stop?

6. Does the sensation have movement to it or a vibration? Does it have temperature or color?

7. Continue watching this sensation. As thoughts appear, return your attention to the sensation at hand. If thoughts try to hook you, say thank you to your mind and return your attention to the sensation.

8. Try putting a hand on this sensation, softly feeling the weight and warmth of your hand. This is not to soothe the feeling away, but to send love and compassion both to your body and to this feeling, no matter the discomfort.

9. Imagine you are holding this sensation like you would hold a crying child or a scared animal.

10. Continue observing this sensation.

11. When you are ready, zoom your attention out to the rest of your body. Notice your breath, once again, as it flows in and out. Notice the whole of your body sitting where it is sitting. This sensation is one part of you, but it is not all of you. Notice what your toes feel like, and your fingers and ears. There are sensations to be found everywhere.

12. When you are done, slowly open your eyes and continue with your day.

Identify Willingness

MATERIALS: Journal
SUGGESTED TIME: 10 to 15 minutes

Recall that acceptance is the opposite of experiential avoidance, and willingness is acting with an openness to experience any sensation or feeling. When we start to make changes in our lives, difficult emotions show up, and our urge to avoid also appears. This exercise will help you identify what experiences will likely show up and allow you to identify actions that you are willing to take, given the sensations that might appear.

1. Think of something you have been avoiding. It does not have to be your most feared experience, but something of moderate intensity. For example, if you have a heights phobia, you might choose a movie you have wanted to watch that involves heights, or going to an office that is a few stories up.

2. I invite you to start small, because our attempt to get freedom in life is like learning to mountain climb. If you are just starting out, you would not start to climb Mount Kilimanjaro. You might start with local hiking and mountain climbing gyms, then try out spots in Yosemite or in the Grand Canyon before trying a huge mountain.

3. Once you have identified your action, take a few minutes to write about why you want to do it. Has it been meaningful in the past? Is it connected to an important relationship? Does it represent a version of yourself that you are trying to become? Your responses will touch on values and set a wonderful stage for values work in future chapters. For now, don't worry about specificity or justifying this action, simply get in touch with the vitality of the action.

Continued

4. Take a moment to imagine this action. Paint the picture in your mind. Now label and write all the thoughts, memories, emotions, sensations, and urges that come up. Write for about 10 minutes. It is helpful to stop when you get stuck and reimagine the scenario until new content appears.

5. Now spend a couple moments considering if you are willing to experience these thoughts, sensations, and emotions if you do this action. They may not show up; we don't know that yet. Just ask yourself if you are willing to experience them. Willingness is like taking a jump. There is no "in-between"—you either jump or you stay on the ground. However, you do get to decide the height of the jump. You can jump down a small step or out of an airplane with a parachute. Your willingness cannot be conditional, but you can set parameters. You might be willing to take the elevator up to the high floor and take it right back down. You might watch a video taken at a high height for 10 minutes. Either way, you are choosing to be 100 percent present with whatever shows up.

6. Now write out your commitment. If you gave your action time parameters, know that you can continue to sit with whatever is present after the time is "up," but that you are also free to leave then. Either way, you are practicing acceptance and willingness for your emotions and sensations for the time you committed to.

Looking for a Passenger

MATERIALS: Journal
SUGGESTED TIME: Varies

Let's return to our Passengers on the Bus metaphor (page 50) for this exercise. Recall that life is like driving a bus full of passengers that represent our thoughts, emotions, memories, urges, and sensations. We will use that metaphor to practice acceptance of some of your emotions and sensations by seeing them as passengers along for the ride of life.

Consider an action you want to take that might bring up something painful. If you are completing each exercise in order, you might choose a different action than the one you chose in the previous chapter. This is where you want to steer your bus. Examples include: having a painful and honest conversation with someone, researching academic programs to begin the process of returning to school, or going to an event to meet new people.

1. Imagine pointing your bus toward that action lane. Imagine yourself taking the action.

2. What passengers, specifically emotions and sensations, show up?

3. You might notice that some passengers come with thoughts. For example, Fear might show up with sensations of butterflies in the stomach and say, "You'll fail. You'll make a fool of yourself. You'll mess everything up." Notice what each passenger has to say, and respond: "Okay, thank you, Passenger."

4. Ask yourself: "Am I willing to continue driving toward this action with Fear along for the ride? Do I want to go to class or meet someone while Fear is present in my body and mind?" If your response is "yes," then continue to find

Continued

other passengers. Maybe Rapid Heartbeat shows up, or Overwhelmed.

5. Then, once again, ask each passenger what they have to say. Ask them what they feel like. Then, ask yourself if you are willing to bring them along on the bus to your destination. You do not have to want them there. Just ask yourself if you are willing to take this action with this passenger present.

6. If at any point, you answer "No, I am not willing to bring this passenger along," ask yourself what the costs are of not doing this action. Explore the costs of fighting with this passenger. When have you fought this passenger before? How did it go? When have you listened to this passenger and stayed on Safe Street? How has that worked to bring you here? Do you want to stay on Safe Street? Are you willing to give up this part of your life to this passenger?

7. Remind yourself that these questions are not intended to force you to accept this passenger and grit your teeth through your action. They are meant to help you see how important this action is.

8. If you are still struggling to make space for passengers, consider the option in the last exercise: Is there an amount of time or smaller activity that would make you willing? If you are unwilling to bring this passenger to improv class, are you willing to go to class for five minutes? Are you willing to go and bring a friend? Are you willing to go to a different class?

9. The more we seek out actions that are important to us *and* bring up our passengers, the more opportunities we have to learn to befriend them and allow them in our lives. Practice taking actions that bring up passengers, such as skipping dessert or coffee, greeting strangers, or taking new routes to work or home.

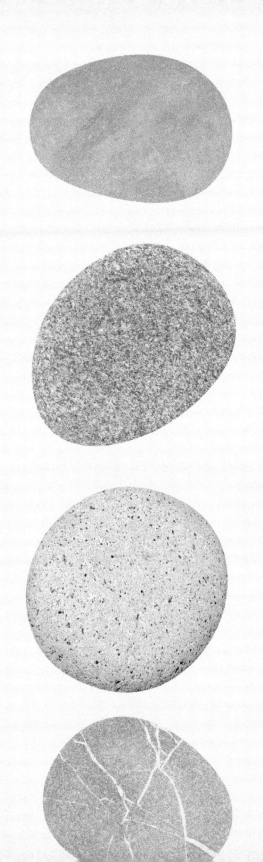

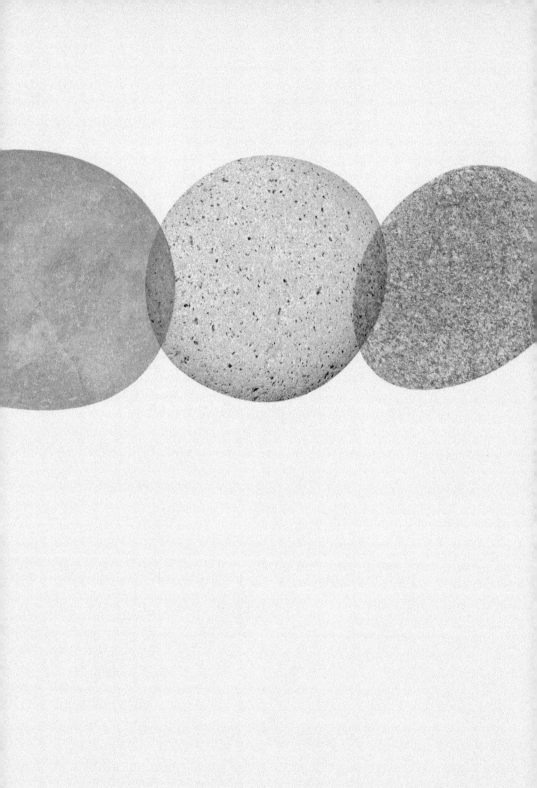

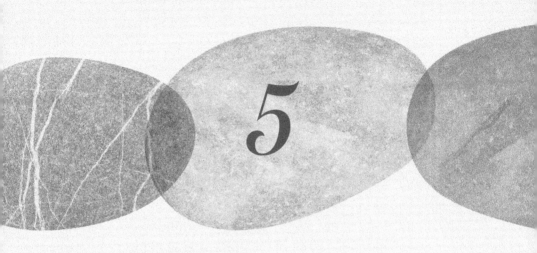

5

CONTACTING
THE PRESENT

Contacting the present moment is necessary to use any ACT skill. Defusing from thoughts, sitting with emotions, or moving toward what is important to us all take awareness of the present. In fact, presence and the observing self (which will be discussed in chapter 6) encompass both sides of ACT. The acceptance side of ACT includes presence, observing self, defusion, and acceptance, while the commitment side includes presence, observing self, values, and committed action. While all the skills are necessary for change, presence and observing self link the skills together.

In this chapter, I will describe what presence, or mindfulness, is, especially in the context of ACT. You might remember from chapter 2 that mindfulness can be taught in meditation, but that meditation is not a requirement of ACT (see page 25). To that end, I will include various exercises, some of which are formal practices and others that you can do as you move through your day. You will also see another case example to see how these skills have affected people I have worked with. Remember to practice presence each day, so that it can change the relationship you have with your mind.

Behind the Method

Imagine walking to a beautiful vista overlooking the sun setting in the distance. Take a moment to imagine the scene—soak in the colors, the changing light, the song of birds, the breeze rifling through your hair.

The awe that many of us experience in situations like this is only experienced in the present. When we are fully enveloped in a scene such as this, our problem-solving minds are quieter. It is unlikely someone would say, "I just wish there was more pink in that sunset." Instead, we fully experience it, just as it is. A bit of pain is usually found in the tenderest of moments, and the joy experienced in this moment is often a bit bittersweet. For example, I often experience longing or a bit of sadness along with joy and gratitude. Being fully present means allowing the whole experience with wonder and curiosity. What if we could all see our lives as the sunsets they are?

Because anxiety takes us into problem solving and the future, effectively taking our attention elsewhere, we often miss out on wonderful moments like this. However, presence and awareness are for the difficult moments in our lives as well as the beautiful sunsets. We cannot bring skills into the present until we are aware that we are hooked by thoughts or avoiding a sensation. If you are trying to conquer anxiety behaviors, presence will allow you to see the situation as it really is, instead of as your mind says it is. Learning only occurs in the present, so any work on anxiety requires mindfulness.

Take the example of Jake, who had a fear of driving. He would experience a wave of anxiety that would make his mind think that he was frozen, and the thought "I can't drive. I am going to get us in an accident" would cross his mind. When he started practicing awareness, he noticed that the feeling of being frozen was a construction of his mind. While it felt very real, he noticed he could physically move his limbs while driving. He was also able to notice the thought that he would cause an accident while he continued driving safely. By becoming present with his anxiety, he defused from thoughts, allowed emotions, and could drive safely. As he practiced this, the anxious thoughts became less and less real and the anxiety diminished.

In this chapter, you will learn various ways to practice becoming flexibly present. Flexible is key here. Practice these skills in various activities so that you are able to bring them to any situation. Common misconceptions will also be discussed, because awareness and mindfulness can be difficult to use flexibly and effectively.

Presence Techniques

The following techniques include metaphors and techniques to practice getting present. Try practicing these throughout your day and notice what happens to your attention.

Awareness Is like a Flashlight

A great metaphor to help you along your presence journey is to think of your attention as a flashlight beam. Imagine you are walking along a path, in the dark, with your flashlight. While you cannot control what you see with your flashlight, you are able to control where you shine it. You would want to use a flexible, sweeping motion with your flashlight to see the path ahead and to be aware of any obstacles or creatures in the way. If you hear a noise, you might turn on your flashlight and fix it on the source of the noise for some time. It would not be effective to keep your flashlight rigidly focused on the path ahead of you if you hear noise to your right, nor would it be effective to keep the flashlight shining off the path for too long. Similarly, we cannot control what we think, feel, or sense with our five senses, but we can choose where to put our attention. Ignoring something important is a bit like not shining our flashlight on a noise; it does not make it go away. Moving the flashlight flexibly and intentionally allows us to respond effectively.

Passengers on the Bus

Recall the Passengers on the Bus metaphor (see page 50), in which passengers represent your emotions, sensations, and memories. Contacting the present is like being aware of your position in the driver's seat, awareness of where you are driving while observing your passengers.

Follow the Breath

This is a simple exercise at the root of many mindfulness apps and practices. Simply set a timer and follow your breath. Even 10 minutes is beneficial. When your mind wanders, which it inevitably will, note *thinking* on *feeling*, then return to your breath. I find it helpful to count 1 on inhale, 2 on exhale, and so on until 10, when I go back to 1 and continue.

Watching the breath can increase anxiety about breathing for some. Fortunately, there are many different exercises to try! I have also found that that anxiety improves as I watch my breath, noting my mind's reactions as I go.

Three Breath Check-In

This is a great exercise to do throughout the day. At any point in your day, stop what you are doing, take three breaths, and notice what you feel in your body and what your mind is saying. You might place these check-ins at significant moments in your day to help you remember—before every meeting, before or after a meal, each time you go to the restroom. This exercise can help you bring mindful attention into your everyday life.

Feeling the Senses

Sensation is inherently in the present, so noticing your five senses is an easy way to get present wherever you are.

- Notice what you can see without searching for something to look at. Do not just notice objects; notice lighting, shadows, the spaces between objects.

- Then notice sound. Notice the obvious sounds like music or talking, but also attend to faraway sounds like birds or construction.

- Notice smells. Again, attend to softer smells as well.

- Notice taste, even if it is a neutral taste.

- Finally, notice bodily sensations. Start on the outside. Where do you feel yourself touching the surfaces you are around? Then move inside. What do you feel in your chest, stomach, legs, arms?

Mindful Communication

Often when we are communicating with someone, we are focused on our own mind—the stories it spins, what we want to say next, our own nervousness or frustration if the conversation is difficult. Mindful communication is about resting your attention in the conversation itself, rather than your mind's stories *about* the conversation.

Next time you are in a conversation, focus your attention on the other person. Notice the sound of their voice and their words, then focus on their facial expression. Switch between what you can see and what you can hear a few times. Then, try to hold both what you can hear and see at the same time. Your mind will generate relations while they talk; that is normal! Just return your focus to what they are saying and doing.

Lane's Experience with Presence

Lane came to see me to address her anxiety. She had experienced trauma and a neglectful home growing up and was noticing its effects on her life now. She was a perfectionist to the point of being self-critical of any mistakes, worried frequently about her decisions, and felt used in relationships because she did not speak her mind out of anxiety. We used mindfulness throughout our work together.

For Lane, getting present with sensations and thoughts changed her relationship with herself. She was able to notice reactions to others, giving her clues to her needs, which allowed her to be more active in relationships. Becoming present with self-criticism allowed her to defuse from the criticism itself, and sit with the fear of not having a secure life. She discovered that her perfectionism was rooted in insecurity. She was terrified of not being enough in others' eyes, as well as not *having* enough to survive. Her pursuit to be perfect in college and work was to control the uncertainty of others' reactions, plus the whims of a shaky economy.

Practicing presence did not eliminate these fears, and it certainly did not eliminate the reality of many people in Lane's situation of economic insecurity. Presence allowed Lane to open up to these fears, to get curious about them, and then act with what was workable and in line with her values. She became more vulnerable with people and more self-compassionate. She turned in assignments even when they were not perfect, and asked her boss for help. Instead of revealing her as a fraud, these actions proved to be more workable for Lane, bringing her closer to her community and mentors. She was also able to get real about her finances, making decisions that set her up for the long term, while allowing her to enjoy simple pleasures. Instead of using deprivation to manage her finances, she used her values.

As you practice mindfulness, you might notice that the present can become a space to reset. You can stop, notice your internal experience, and decide the next path. Awareness allowed Lane to defuse from and accept internal experiences, remember her values, and recommit to her goals.

Misconceptions

Rigidity often occurs when people struggle with mindfulness or presence. One misconception is that we must practice awareness all the time. Remember that flexibility and workability are our goals. Research published in *Neuropsychologica* found that people who daydreamed most when asked to lie down in an MRI machine scored higher on creative and intellectual ability. If daydreaming is workable, say when you are taking a walk or sitting on your porch in the evening, then there is no need to rigidly bring attention to your breathing in that moment.

Awareness can also be used rigidly when it is guided to an unworkable area of life. For example, John experienced anxiety in relationships. When he needed to give feedback to his employees, he became anxious at their reactions. He had been using mindfulness for a long time, and thought to pay attention to his breathing while giving feedback, but he noticed that he was focusing on his breath to reduce his anxiety. When he shifted his attention to the facial expression and nonverbal cues of who he was talking to, he noticed that he was more present to the conversation, more open to both his and his employees' emotions, and able to communicate more effectively.

Mindfulness and awareness can also be used as distraction. Notice if you are only attending to neutral or positive stimuli; a situation calls us to be present with our own or someone else's suffering or pain at times. Mindful attention to the body or sounds in that moment may actually serve as distraction. Similarly, some people's commitment to meditation practices can lead to using meditation to distract, avoid difficult conversations, or focus on one's own internal experience. Presence is not an inherently self-centered exercise, but it can be used in a self-centered way. Effective presence allows us to respond to the current situation in a way that aligns with our values as the person we most want to be.

The following exercises will allow you to practice contacting the present. These are formal practices designed to help you freely move your attention to the present. I recommend that you practice each a few times. I also recommend that you practice getting present at least once a day. You might choose to do one exercise daily or cycle through all the exercises.

Mindful Eating

MATERIALS: Clock or timer
SUGGESTED TIME: 2 minutes

Anxiety can produce eating problems—either eating too much or not eating enough. This exercise will help you practice presence and awareness. It may also help you regulate eating behaviors; when we slow down and focus on the sensations of eating, we often listen to our body's hunger and fullness cues. It is also a great daily meditation for those who want options beyond following the breath.

The first few times you do this exercise, pick a small item to eat: a raisin, a piece of popcorn, or a small piece of fruit. Spend 10 to 20 seconds, which is about two to four breaths, on each prompt.

1. Set the timer for 2 minutes.

2. First, hold the item in your hand, noticing texture, light, and color.

3. Now roll it between your fingers, noticing the sensation of touch. Explore the texture and any grooves in your piece of food.

4. Bring it close to your mouth. This time notice the sensation of smell. Continuing moving it around, noticing if the smell changes.

5. Place the item in your mouth. Do not bite down quite yet. Just notice sensations in your mouth. You might notice salivation, the urge to start eating. Also notice what it feels like to have this piece of food in your mouth.

6. Now, very slowly, begin chewing. Notice the bursts of flavor when you chew, and pause between each chew to notice the changes of taste and sensation. Notice an urge to swallow and what it is like to slowly eat this piece of food. Do not swallow yet.

7. Finally, as you finish chewing, swallow the mouthful, and notice what that feels like. Try to follow the sensations as the food move down your throat, chest, or stomach.

8. Sit for a moment, noticing any change in your body. Notice the lingering taste in your mouth, sensations in your stomach, or continued salivation.

Because this exercise takes only a couple of minutes, you have a few options for incorporating it in your life. You might do this exercise once a day with a small piece of food. You could also do this for the first bite of every meal. You might do a concentrated exercise with one bite, and keep that mindful awareness as you start eating at a more normal pace. This exercise often slows our habit of eating rapidly, which can help you stay engaged with your body's signal of fullness.

Mindful Movement

MATERIALS: None
SUGGESTED TIME: 10 minutes

Mindful walking is a common meditation technique. I will describe a way to practice mindful walking here, then extrapolate to other mindful movement.

I recommend doing this exercise for at least 10 minutes daily for a few days before adjusting it. This will help you understand and experience the basics of the exercise, so that incorporating it into your daily life keeps the benefits.

1. Start by standing still. Feel your weight in your feet. Notice where the weight is placed. Notice the muscles in your calves, thighs, stomach, and glutes holding you up. Notice your shoulders and arms as they rest by your side.

2. Prepare to take your first step. Notice how you shift your weight into one leg.

3. Notice your heel lift off the ground, rolling through your toes, and lifting off your other foot. Notice the feeling of your knee bending, your thigh engaging.

4. Notice your leg swing forward, the calf muscle engaging.

5. As your heel touches the ground again, notice your weight shifting onto this leg as your foot rolls onto the ground.

6. Notice how, as your weight shifts, your other heel will start to lift. Notice both legs holding weight as one foot plants and the other lifts.

7. Notice the lifting foot now—how it lifts, swings your leg forward, and plants again.

8. In this exaggerated fashion, take several steps, noticing the weight shifting from one foot to the other, noticing muscles engaging in turn.

9. You might speed up your pace just a touch, while remaining slow. Notice the fluidity of these weight shifts and muscle engagements. Notice the rolling sensation of walking more fluidly.

10. Ten minutes of this exercise might take you just from one end of your space to another and back. That's okay!

11. You might choose to walk a slow, but close to normal, pace. Continue to notice how your weight shifts from one leg to another, as you notice the sensations of your leg and the bottoms of your feet.

After practicing this exercise very slowly several times, you might adapt it to other activities. If you are a runner, you might notice the rapid weight changes in your feet. You might pick one foot and notice what it feels like for it to lift up and return to the ground repeatedly, then switch feet, then notice both simultaneously. You can do the same practice as you walk to work.

You can also bring mindful attention to any movement. As you clean your space, you might notice muscles and points of contact as you clean floors or scrub a dish.

Remember that this is not thinking *about* moving. It is simply witnessing movement. This practice, over time, will help you be more present in your body.

Body Scan Meditation

MATERIALS: None
SUGGESTED TIME: Varies

Body scans are a common mindfulness technique. Practicing scanning your body will help you notice sensations and emotions. Recall that in the last chapter, one of the acceptance exercises had a mini body scan in it to help you find the sensation associated with an emotion. Regular body scan practice can help you attend to and welcome sensations, whether they are associated with an emotion or physical pain.

You can record these prompts, or remember them and do them on your own. When you first begin, linger at each prompt for a couple of breaths. As you practice, you might find that a slower cadence works for you.

1. Begin by lying down flat on your back. You can close your eyes or keep them unfocused on the ceiling. If you find yourself falling asleep regularly during this practice, try it sitting up in a relaxed but alert posture.

2. Start with your head. Notice sensations on your scalp.

3. Notice your eyes, the space between your eyebrows, and your temple.

4. Notice your ears.

5. Notice your cheeks and nose.

6. What do you feel in your mouth? In your lips?

7. Notice your jaw.

8. Move down your neck, observing sensations.

9. Now move to your upper chest and shoulders.

10. Move your attention to your left arm. Notice your upper arm, then your forearm.

11. Notice your wrist, hand, and each finger separately.

12. Repeat on the right side, noticing the upper arm and forearm.

13. What do you feel in your right wrist, hand, and fingers?

14. Start again at your chest and move slowly, smoothly down.

15. Notice sensations in your mid-chest.

16. Notice your stomach and abdomen.

17. Notice your back and lower back.

18. Observe sensations in your pelvis, hips, and buttocks.

19. Move down your thighs, noticing sensations in your upper legs.

20. Notice your knees.

21. What do you feel in your lower legs, both calves and shins?

22. Notice your ankles.

23. Move down your feet slowly.

24. What do you notice at the top of your feet?

25. What do you notice at your heel?

26. Observe the balls of your feet.

27. Notice each toe.

28. Now expand your awareness to your whole body, holding your entire body and all its sensations in your awareness.

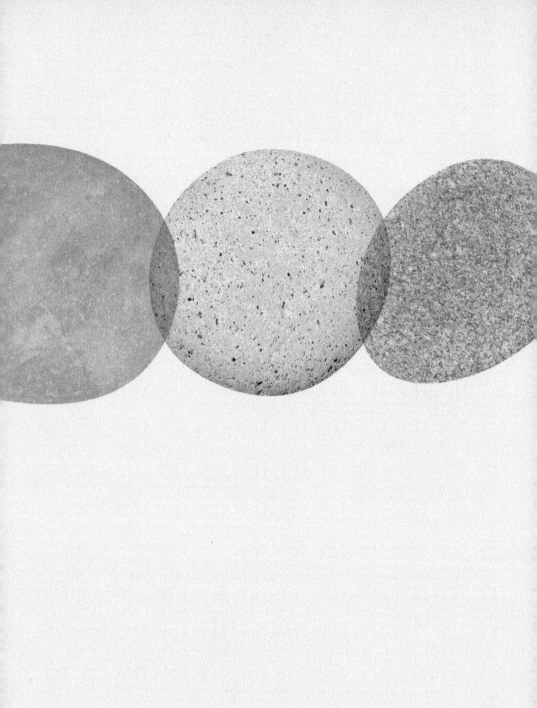

6

THE OBSERVING SELF

n this chapter, we build off the presence skills from chapter 5 and go further, by noticing the part of ourselves that observes the present. Simply put, as you notice your experiences, you can connect with the part of you that is doing the noticing. This is your observing self.

Being in contact with the observer self has multiple benefits. First, it acts as defusion from thoughts about who you are. If you can observe these thoughts, then you are not bound by them. It also provides a safe space to experience difficult emotions, as I will explain further. Finally, getting in contact with your observer self will give you a great foundation to go into values and committed action in the following chapters.

In this chapter, I will explain the benefits of the observing self, how to differentiate it from the thinking self, and provide many metaphors and exercises to help you connect with this part of yourself. While all the ACT skills are inherently experiential, this is particularly true of the observing self. It is immune to intellectual thought. It must be experienced. Even calling the observing self an *it* is misleading, as it is not an object. So while I try to explain it and talk about it, it is very important that you experience the observing self through exercises and metaphors.

Behind the Method

The observing self is beyond our mind's judgments, evaluations, and stories. For that reason, contacting the observing self allows us to defuse from our mind's judgments about ourselves. This allows us to have other options. Imagine your mind has decided that you are An Anxious Person. Anxious People do not go for promotions at work, meet new people, or move across the country. If you contact your observing self, however, you will find that you are just a person, and a person can do any of those actions.

As I discussed in chapter 1, a significant process of anxiety is the fear of our own experiences. When we fear a racing heart, painful memories, or judgments, we start to limit our lives to avoid anything that could trigger those experiences. What if you could have those experiences and feel safe? What would it be like to safely hold terror, panic, or despair?

Having a safe space to experience difficult emotions means that we are no longer in danger of the experience. People often describe fearing that anxiety will take them over—a sense of being powerless in the face of the fear. I recall someone describing to me their fear of exploring an anxious topic as a feeling that they would explode or be demolished, saying: "I know that I won't die, but it feels like I might, you know? Like I'll just curl up in a ball and explode if I let the anxiety go." It would be almost impossible to experience a full life if you are avoiding that level of pain.

The observing self allows us to experience pain in a way that never makes the pain larger than ourselves. We can see it as one part of us. Tapping into this observing self, for instance, I can see the shiver of panic move over my spine, while also noticing my feet on the floor and the smell of grass. No longer does that shiver of panic mean certain demise.

The observing self also allows us to cultivate self-acceptance. Many clients come to me asking to improve their self-esteem or to have more confidence. This often means having more positive thoughts about ourselves. As previous chapters might have taught you, this is not a helpful answer. For every "I am a great person" thought, the opposite "I am a terrible person" thought is at the ready. Furthermore, none of us are consistent humans. If I believe I am only a warm and kind person, I will miss all the ways that I can be cold or cruel. I might even be resistant to others' feedback about my behavior, making it harder for me to move toward my values of warmth and kindness!

Self-acceptance means seeing your behavior as it is and accepting the difficult emotions or reactions that arise as a result. Ironically, this practice of opening up to our full selves allows us to move closer to our values. When we close ourselves off from our demons, we have no way of working with them.

THINKING SELF AND OBSERVING SELF

When we first begin to acquire language, we start by hearing our caregivers talk to us. Then, we begin speaking back. Caregivers often narrate the world to their young children, as in the following example: "There's Daddy! He is cleaning. Look at Daddy cleaning." There is a listener–the child–and a speaker–the parent. As children begin speaking, these roles switch back and forth. At some point, we begin this same process internally, and our inner voice is born. We don't have to say "There is a dog" out loud any longer; we can simply think it–or, even quicker, notice the dog and make quick connections to memories of a dog or thoughts about dogs.

Throughout this process, we never lose the listener and the speaker. When once we shared the listener/speaker roles with caregivers, we now internalize both roles. Your thinking self, or mind, plays the role of speaker. It narrates, makes connections, makes judgments, recalls previous events, predicts future events, and so on. The listener simply listens. It is nonjudgmental and simply receives the dialogue. Because the speaker is so active, we often mistake our whole self for that incessant speaker. When we can get in contact with the listener, we can see our minds as what they are: speakers telling one version of the story. Our observing self allows us to zoom out from that story and see the possibility of other stories and perspectives.

Observing Self Techniques

The following metaphors and techniques will help you contact the observing self and understand its perspective. Because this is a difficult concept to understand intellectually, metaphors are the best way to experience this part of ourselves.

Blue Sky

You can think of your observing self as the blue sky spreading out in all directions, and your sensations, emotions, and thoughts as the weather. Some days there are slow moving clouds, and other days it might seem like a hurricane is sweeping over the sky. Either way, the sky is above the clouds. It cannot be harmed by the weather. It holds all the weather, and yet is not the weather. Your observing self similarly cannot be hurt by your experience, and acts as a container for all experiences. Notice the weather in any given moment and try to notice the sky.

Passengers on the Bus (Reprise)

Recall the Passengers on the Bus metaphor (see page 50). You might remember my claim that this metaphor of you driving a bus full of passengers that represent thoughts, feelings, and memories contains all the elements of ACT. You can think of the observing self as the bus itself. It holds all these experiences. It bears witness to our internal world. Yet it is not hurt or affected by the passengers. It remains the same if the passengers are all yelling or if they are quiet.

Courtroom Drama Metaphor (Reprise)

Another metaphor I used earlier in the book was the courtroom drama (see page 41). It feels especially helpful when your mind is arguing or debating, even over something as simple as the mental struggle many of us have getting out of bed in the morning. If each side of the argument is represented by the sides of a court, the observing self might be the courtroom itself. It holds the experience. The observing self might also be a court reporter, who listens and observes the thoughts and feelings without taking a side.

Observe the Observer

To get in touch with your observing self, start by noticing your present experience. The observing self can only be found in the present. Then observe the part of you that observes your experience. "There is my breath. And there's the part of me noticing my breath." The moment you do this, your mind might jump into analysis. Simply observe those thoughts, then notice the observer.

I Can't

Anxiety can have a limiting effect for many people. Dreams and goals are cast aside because the mind says, "I can't do that." One way to contact the observer self is to play with these thoughts. Start simple. Say in your mind, "I can't walk around this room." Then walk around while thinking that thought. Next, choose something you have been neglecting, that your mind says you cannot do. Practice this action while thinking "I can't," and notice the part of you that holds both the action and the thought.

Gabrielle's Experience of the Observing Self

Gabrielle came to me for chronic depression. When we first started working together, I noticed that she seemed to spend much of her time trying to talk me into believing her self-stories. These self-stories ranged from "I am selfish" to "I am a terrible burden on everyone around me." When we tried to do acceptance or values work, these passengers reared their heads and stopped Gabrielle from feeling anything other than sadness and shame.

Using a combination of defusion and observing self skills, Gabrielle learned to see herself as more than just self-stories. She did not dispute them, but instead held them lightly. She allowed the possibility of being more than just a burden. She learned to come back to her observing self through mindfulness practices when in pain. This allowed her to feel emotions without defense. Through this process, she learned about her needs in relationships, as well as her values. Self-stories had cut her off from anything important to her. It is impossible to have dreams when you believe you are a burden.

From this space, Gabrielle was able to explore trauma, including racial injustices she had experienced. She returned to this space as a refuge while experiencing grief, anger, and fear. She was able to connect with multiple roles in her life. She could be a student, a teacher, a daughter, a sister, a friend, an enemy, a neighbor, an advocate. None of these alone defined her. She could recognize when she was unkind, without the selfish story flooding her with shame too intense to do anything. When she recognized she had moved away from her values of compassion, she would accept that moment and pivot back. She became more vulnerable, gentler, and more open to others' feedback.

Misconceptions

Observing self is one of the hardest skills for me to teach. It is resistant to intellectual understanding, and the more I try to explain it, the harder it gets to understand. If you are grappling with this concept, you are not alone! Keep trying the exercises. When your mind says "I get it!" try them again.

The observing self is not about picking the right self-story or identity. It simply holds those stories and identities and watches them come up. Therefore, the observing self is not a thought. This is where it can get really hard to explain. If I observe my thinking and say to myself, "Ahh, and that's the observing self," those words are more thoughts. The observing self is the part of me that can witness my first thoughts as well as the part of me that observed the thought "Ahh, and that's the observing self." If my mind gets smug and thinks, "I've really got this observing self stuff down!" my observer self will be right there observing those thoughts.

Some people who have experience with dissociation, or the experience of being outside of reality, struggle to diffcrentiate it from the observing self. An ACT therapist can help you more specifically with this concern, but here are some differences I have found.

First, sometimes people experience extreme judgments while dissociating; they describe a sense of watching themselves with contempt. The observing self is free of judgment. It is also not outside of your experience. When you think of the blue sky, the observing self is right there with the weather, bearing witness to it nonjudgmentally, and being unharmed. Dissociation also serves to get people out of their emotional experience. Because mindfulness and the observer self are so linked, we are often very much in our experience, as painful as it might be, but from a position of safety and observation.

These exercises will help you practice contacting your observing self through journaling and meditation. Try each exercise and notice your experience. Practice contacting your observing self as much as you can, but at least daily.

I am...

MATERIALS: Journal
SUGGESTED TIME: Varies

This exercise, adapted from Dr. Steven C. Hayes, is especially helpful for difficult self-stories that are limiting you. This exercise is not to correct self-stories or find new ones. It is simply about playing with how we view ourselves.

When we do observing self exercises, our mind often gets very active. After all, we are breaking down the mind's power. If you notice yourself getting hooked, pause and do a defusion exercise from chapter 3. Even saying "My mind is having the thought that . . ." a couple of times can be enough to unhook and continue with the exercise.

I will include an example below of the finished exercise.

1. First, complete the following sentences with two of your least favorite qualities, and a quality you want to believe about yourself:

    a. I am _____

    b. I am _____

    c. I am _____

2. Sit with those words for a few minutes. Close your eyes and say the words very slowly. Put a breath between each word and notice what arises in your body and mind. Do emotions flood up? Does your mind start arguing with its own "I am" statements? Just notice.

3. Rewrite your three sentences, and put "or not" at the end. Sit with those words for a minute. Close your eyes and say the sentence slowly with the "or not" at the end. Notice what comes up.

4. Write "I am." Let that simple sentence sit with you. Close your eyes and say the two words slowly a few times. Notice what comes up. Notice how it feels to have this simpler idea of yourself.

5. Now, turn your first "I am" statements into specific behavioral statements by writing "When [situation and/or behavior happens], I feel [quality you chose earlier]."

6. Again, sit with these statements for a few moments, noticing what comes up. Notice emotions as well as thoughts.

If you experienced a sense of ease, possibility, or a more whole self, then you experienced the observing self. It is outside of rigid stories and identities. It might show up differently for you, but when you feel a sense of flexibility and change, you might be getting closer to your observing self.

Here is Gabrielle's experience:

-   I am selfish.
-   I am lazy.
-   I am smart.

Gabrielle noticed her mind arguing for and against them like the courtroom drama. When she said them slowly ("I . . . Am . . . Selfish . . ."), she noticed them as words, but then her mind would start working to prove and disprove the statements.

Continued

I am... continued

Then Gabrielle changed each statement and repeated the meditative exercise.

- I am selfish, or not.

- I am lazy, or not.

- I am smart, or not.

Gabrielle noticed that her mind continued to argue, but it seemed more distant. She noticed a small sense of freedom. When she said, "I . . . Am . . . Smart . . . Or . . . Not . . ." she noticed a sense of relief. While this was a prized quality, it also gave her a lot of pressure to never not be smart. She now saw that she could have smart moments and not-so-smart moments.

Then Gabrielle wrote "I AM" in large letters and repeated the meditation exercise. Gabrielle noticed some mental confusion; her mind really wanted to answer who she was. However, she again connected with a sense of ease and being.

Finally, Gabrielle made more specific behavior statements for each quality.

- When I do not want to talk to my sister about her work problems, I feel selfish.

- When I do not complete my work by the end of the day, I feel lazy.

- When I help one of my coworkers with a work problem, I feel smart.

Gabrielle found a greater sense of ease when she saw these qualities as self-stories that arose in certain situations.

Continuous You

MATERIALS: None
SUGGESTED TIME: Varies

This meditation technique gets into more direct contact with the observing self. It is adapted from an exercise by ACT trainer Russ Harris.

You can record, or have a friend record, these prompts, or you can find similar recordings in the resources section. Keep several breaths between each prompt.

- Get in a comfortable position.

- With your eyes open, gaze at something in your space. Look at its colors, texture, shape, how the lighting falls on it. Notice that if you can observe that object, you cannot be that object.

- Notice the part of you watching that object. You have seen many objects in your life, but this part of you watching them has always been the same.

- Let your gaze become unfocused or close your eyes. Notice where your body touches the floor. Notice your body as it rests in this space.

- Now, notice that if you can observe your body, you cannot be your body. This body has changed over the years from an infant to a child to an adolescent to an adult. Even smaller changes happen every year. Yet, the part of you that can observe your body is unchanged.

- If your mind gets going, notice that, thank your mind, and continue with the exercise.

- Now notice your breathing. Watch the inhale and exhale.

- Watch your inhale and notice the short pause at the top of the inhale before you start exhaling. Notice the pause at the

Continued

bottom of an exhale before you start inhaling. Watch these little pauses for several breath cycles.

◆ Notice that if you can observe your breathing, you cannot be your breathing. If your mind starts thinking, just come back to your breath.

◆ Notice the part of you watching your breathing. Notice that even when your breathing has been slower or faster, that part of you has remained the same.

◆ Now, notice your thoughts. They may have gotten spinning after the last prompt, or they might just be circling around the same old thoughts. Watch them for a few moments.

◆ Notice that if you can observe your thoughts, you cannot be your thoughts.

◆ Notice the part of you that can notice thoughts. This same part of you could notice the thoughts you had when you were a teen or a child.

◆ Now shift your attention to a sensation or feeling. Watch this feeling for a few moments. Observe where it is in your body and how it moves. Notice that if you can observe this feeling, you cannot be this feeling.

◆ Notice the part of you that can observe this feeling. Your body has experienced many sensations and emotions, yet this part of you that can observe them has remained the same.

◆ Now, observe the entirety of your present experience. Sit and be present with whatever comes up.

◆ As you do so, notice the part of you that is observing. Come back to watching your experience, then notice the watcher again.

◆ After several moments, come back to the room, noticing sounds and your body sitting where it sits, and slowly open your eyes.

Observing with Compassion

MATERIALS: None
SUGGESTED TIME: Varies

This exercise, adapted from Dr. Steven C. Hayes's *A Liberated Mind*, can be used when you are struggling with some kind of pain. It involves presence, acceptance, and observing self.

    You can record, or have a friend record, these prompts. Take several breaths between each prompt.

- Get in a comfortable but alert position. To start, watch your breathing for a few cycles. Get present in the moment and in your body.

- Scan your body to find where you are holding a painful emotion. Pay special attention to the chest, stomach, and abdomen. Watch this emotion for a few breaths. Notice its shape, movement, and edges.

- Notice the part of you that can notice this emotion. If your mind starts buzzing at that, come back to the emotion itself, then again notice the part of you noticing.

- When you are connected with the observing self, imagine watching yourself sitting here. You might imagine sitting beside yourself. Notice what your body looks like from this perspective. Also notice that this "me" is suffering on the inside.

- Notice if you experience compassion for this person you are observing. Is this person worthy of compassion?

- If you notice yourself caught up in thinking or feeling, come back to the part of you noticing. Come back to the perspective of the observing self watching your body.

Continued

- ◆ Now, take your observing self to the other side of the room and watch yourself continue to sit there.

- ◆ Consider people nearby, either in your home or in your community, who are suffering now. Do not get caught up in thinking *about* them suffering. Just notice yourself in pain and notice that others might be feeling pain in this very moment.

- ◆ Again, notice if you can experience compassion for this "me" across the room. Is this person worthy of compassion?

- ◆ If you lost contact with your observing self, come back to the part of you noticing this pain, noticing this "me" across the room.

- ◆ Now, imagine that the you from 10 years from now is in the room, watching you experience this pain right now. What might that future you say to present you? Do not feel pressure to answer this question a specific way. Just notice what comes up.

- ◆ Watch yourself in this pain while noticing the advice and compassion coming up.

- ◆ When you are ready, come back to your breathing, to the moment, then open your eyes.

- ◆ Write down the advice from future you.

I do a version of this exercise "on the go" when I experience a bit of pain, and am not in a place to do the full exercise. I observe the pain, notice my observing self, and ask myself, "What would Future Rachel say to you now?" I have internally established that Future Rachel is me several years from now. I have noticed that she is consistently compassionate, loving, and encouraging. She neither admonishes me nor tells me to just eat ice cream to soothe my pain. She is fully present for the pain and encourages me to do the next right thing.

And with that said, the next chapter on values might help you clarify what the next right thing is for you.

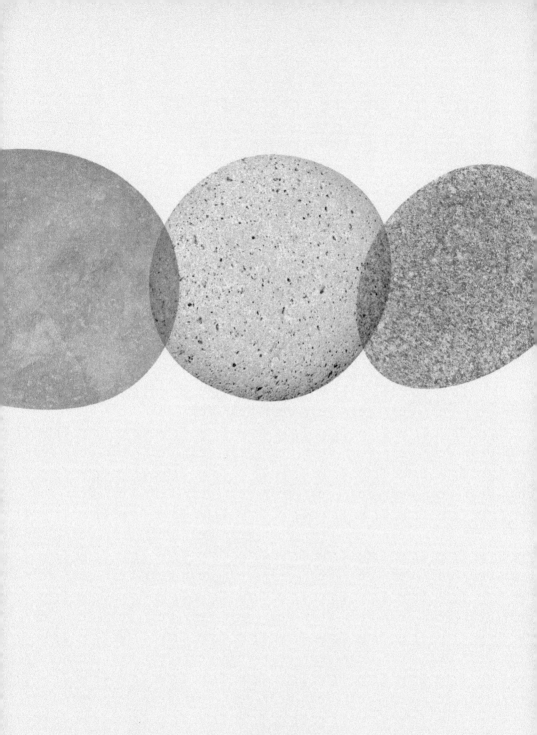

7

VALUES

V alues bring us to the other side of ACT. You may remember from chapter 5 that defusion, acceptance, presence, and observing self are the acceptance side of ACT, while presence, observing self, values, and committed action represent the commitment side (see page 78). One goal of this chapter is to demonstrate how values can move you toward making the changes you wanted to make when you selected this book. Values give all the previous ACT skills meaning.

What is your reason for practicing defusion, acceptance, presence, and self-as-context? If the answer is for anxiety to disappear, then you might want to return to the Problem-Solving in Overdrive section at the end of chapter 2 (see page 32). If your reason for practicing these skills is to be brave, be a more engaged parent, contribute to the world through art or business, or connect more deeply with others, you are already doing values work. In ACT, we do not sit with our present experience out of obligation or an idea of betterment; we show up in pursuit of a grand, vital, meaningful life.

I will describe what values are and give you some metaphors and techniques to start getting a sense of values in your own life. A case study will help you see values in action. Finally, exercises at the end of the chapter will help you identify your values. This is particularly important work to do before moving on to the next chapter.

Behind the Method

Values reflect our deepest desires for how we want to live our lives. Living a life aligned with values leads to greater meaning and vitality, even if it also means encountering painful emotions.

Maybe you have been living life bound to rules and avoidant of emotions. When your mind says, "I can't do that," or "Wait until you are less anxious," you listen. When you feel anxiety, you turn away. This is not a life lived by values. Alternatively, you might live your life according to goals. In this case, "I'll be happy when I get that job" might turn into "I will be happy when I make more money" and "This sense of unease will go away when I am married." It is never enough, because the bar keeps moving.

Values give us a way out of those empty paths. Values are fully in the present. While we might set goals for the future, our actions and how they relate to values happen right now. Let's say Jan values emotional intimacy and connection. She might have a goal to have a deep friendship or be in a lasting partnership. While these are valid goals, they are not in the present. Jan's choice to say hello to a coworker, smile at the barista serving her coffee, and make small talk with a neighbor, however, can bring her closer to her value of connection. While she does the long-term work to build deep relationships, each step that relates to connection will be meaningful.

As shown in the example above, values are not goals. They are qualities of living that capture the person we want to be in our relationships, in our work, and in our bodies. It is also especially important that they are freely chosen and deeply personal. Values are not more rules to follow, or what your caretakers or friends or culture say you should want.

That is not to say that culture does not influence values. It absolutely does and that fact should be honored. I know that autonomy—one of my chosen values—is related to my being a white person raised in the individualist culture of the United States. People from cultures that emphasize collaboration and community might consider autonomy empty and lonely. I also value vulnerability, collaboration, and asking for help, which are not values encouraged by my culture. It might take time for you to discern which cultural values you freely choose and which you will set aside.

Finally, values can capture both what you do and how you do it. This will become clearer as you explore techniques and exercises. Some values—like compassion, being present, or creativity—capture how we want to live more broadly. I might want to bring creativity to my home, my workplace, and all my relationships. Other values capture specific areas of life, like romantic relationships or leisure time. All are helpful! One of the exercises below will have you sort out which values are most important to you in all these areas of life.

Techniques to Identify Values

The following section has metaphors and ideas to get you thinking about values.

GPS Metaphor

This is one of my favorite metaphors, capturing how values orient us in life. Imagine you are taking a road trip and have a GPS system. In this scenario, you want to explore the American Southwest. Depending on where you are coming from, you will set your direction. If you're headed south, you will likely check each day to confirm that you are going in that direction. You might stop at Zion National Park and want to continue to the Grand Canyon, but confirming that you are going south is the only way to know if you are going where you want to go.

Similarly, values are directions. You do not arrive at "south" just like you do not arrive at "compassion." Goals are more specific. Yes, you may head southward with the specific goal of reaching a park or two. They are important stops on the route, but like any good road trip, these stops are a part of the journey.

Passengers on the Bus (Reprise)

We return to the Passengers on the Bus metaphor (see page 50). Recall that the passengers represent internal experiences, like thoughts, emotions, and memories. Your being present is like being in the driver's seat and the bus is your observing self. Values are represented by the direction you steer your bus. You might choose to get on Spirituality Lane, Brave Avenue, or Passion Street. Your passengers come with you wherever you go, but you get to choose the direction.

Role Models

Identify someone you look up to and deeply admire. They could be a close family member, friend, colleague or mentor, a celebrity or world figure, or even a fictional character. Once you have them in your mind, imagine their actions that typically impress and inspire you. Watch them in your mind's eye doing the actions that brought about your admiration. After a few moments, identify what values you imagined.

60th Birthday Party

Imagine your loved ones have thrown you a 60th birthday party. At this party, everyone is being completely honest; no one is saying something out of social pressure. Everyone takes a few minutes to toast you, and share some words about how you have lived your life up to that point and the impact you have had on them.

First, identify a handful of people in your life that would make such a toast at this party—a mix of friends, family, and colleagues is helpful. Now imagine each of them making their toast, and watch them say what you would most like to hear. Afterward, identify values or themes that you heard.

Splitting Open the Rock

Think of your pain as a rock. Maybe this pain is the grief of years lost to anxiety, goals unfinished, relationships neglected. This rock is ugly, with sharp points. Now imagine splitting it open and finding vibrant purple amethyst inside. Our values and anxiety have the same relationship. If you did not care about something, it would not make you anxious. As you practice sitting with your emotions, try to identify the care within. If you are afraid of social situations, it may be because you value connection, authenticity, and emotional intimacy. If you worry about possible catastrophes, perhaps you value living a responsible life.

Sandra's Values

Sandra came to me after years of therapy. She found herself with anxiety, eating issues, and relationship struggles. The processes I have described here—fusion with rules and thoughts, and experiential avoidance—underlay all her concerns. We discussed values early on, to orient therapy. She knew she wanted to be a more supportive and helpful partner, to be brave and able to contribute more in her social justice work, and to be more compassionate to her body.

As we worked through the skills, experiential avoidance, perfectionism (which is often fusion to rules about how to act), and fear of judgment showed up. We worked through traumas that had launched those fears and rules, then worked to use presence, observing self, acceptance, and defusion skills. Whenever we got stuck, coming back to Sandra's values would ground us. For example, one day she was panicking about an awkward interaction with a colleague. Her mind spun about the consequences it would have on her professionally and socially. When I asked her what the brave and compassionate thing to do next would be, she became present and defused from these worries. While it does not always happen so dramatically, values have a powerful way of orienting us to what is important.

As Sandra learned these skills and moved toward her values, she found that bravery was the value that oriented her the most. Bravery meant staying in a difficult and painful conversation with her partner. Bravery meant setting boundaries with chronically abusive family members. Bravery meant speaking up at work and risking being judged. These were not easy experiences. However, Sandra's connection to her value of bravery allowed her to choose these actions with a willingness to experience whatever came up. Fear, sadness, and anger were welcome on Sandra's journey moving toward bravery.

Misconceptions

Our controlling and problem-solving minds can show up around our values. If you have practiced the skills before this, you might not run into these problems. However, I have seen these common misconceptions show up around values, particularly if we do values work early on in therapy.

First, values are not feelings or internal states. Sometimes people will identify values like "I want to be happy," or "I want to be calm," or "I want to be confident." We do not get to choose our internal states much of the time. If you find internal states come up for you when asked about values, ask yourself what you would do or be if you were calm, peaceful, or confident. For Sandra, her original values were around confidence and calmness. When I asked how she would act in her life if she were always confident and calm, she said, "I would be honest with my family when they treat me poorly. I would speak up in meetings and disagree with higher ranked bosses. I would tell my partner when she hurt my feelings." The values here include honesty, bravery, and speaking up. Sandra learned she could choose to be honest and speak up even when she did not feel calm or confident on the inside. Over time, she found that she was perceived as a calm and confident person, even when she was nervous and fearful on the inside.

Values are also not what we want from other people. "I value being respected"; "I value being seen as a leader"; or "I value being liked" are not values because they do not link to direct action, and they are out of our control. Allowing others' perceptions to define our own sense of meaning is a recipe for suffering. If these are coming up for you, first practice some defusion. Then identify if there are actions you do value in this. Do you value being a leader? Do you value respecting others? Maybe you value standing up for yourself when you feel disrespected. You can practice all these behaviors and worry less about how others see you, concerning yourself with how you want to act in the world instead.

The following exercises will help you identify values. Because values reflect what is most important to us, these exercises all use writing to some extent. Try at least one, and ideally all three, to prepare you for the following chapter.

Values Sorting

MATERIALS: Journal or note cards
SUGGESTED TIME: 10 minutes

This exercise, adapted (with appreciation!) from Jenna LeJeune and Jason Luoma of the Portland Psychotherapy Clinic, will help you identify important values from a list. This is not an exhaustive list. It is designed to get you started if naming values seems overwhelming.

Write each value down in a list in your journal. You may also choose to write each value on the front of a note card with the definition on the back.

VALUES	DESCRIPTION
Boldness	Willingness to take risks
Autonomy	Freedom from control; independence
Hard work	Putting effort into tasks
Challenge	Pursuing difficult actions
Self-Control	Showing restraint even in emotional moments
Virtue	Living according to your morals
Honesty	Speaking truthfully and avoiding lying in all forms
Dependability	Being reliable; following through on commitments
Adventure	Seeking out new places, relationships, experiences
Creativity	Having new ideas or concepts

Continued

EXERCISE

VALUES	DESCRIPTION
Openness	Willing to have new experiences or perspectives
Growth	Putting effort into improving, learning, and changing
Beauty	Appreciating beauty and wanting to create beauty
Ecology	Improving and honoring the environment
Health	Taking actions to support physical health
Humor	Appreciating a lighthearted view of world and self
Knowledge	Seeking out and contributing knowledge
Curiosity	Asking questions and seeking new information
Passion	Devoting self to activities, ideas, and people
Rationality	Appreciating and using logic
Simplicity	Emphasizing a pared-down and simple life
Spirituality	Connecting to spiritual beliefs or rituals
Tradition	Connecting to patterns passed down for generations
Commitment	Dedication over time
Responsibility	Following through on obligations; choosing wise and responsible action
Fun	Playfulness
Leisure	Relaxing and enjoying life

VALUES	DESCRIPTION
Non-Conformity	Challenging authority or norms
Authenticity	Acting true to self; being genuine
Connection	Being close to others
Romance	Nurturing romantic love
Emotional Intimacy	Sharing true, vulnerable self with others
Respect	Showing respect to others
Generosity	Giving to others and to valued causes
Compassion	Empathy; concern for others
Peace	Promoting non-violence
Justice	Seeking equality and justice for all
Helpfulness	Serving others
Contribution	Contributing to lasting change or meaning
Problem-Solving	Figuring things out
Piety	Connecting to religious beliefs and traditions
Competition	Competing with others or self
Community	Contributing to and receiving care from group
Designing/ Creating	Creating new things
Security	Maintaining secure life for self and family

Continued

EXERCISE

VALUES	DESCRIPTION
Loyalty	Staying connected and true to others
Loving	Being affectionate and caring to others
Competent	Developing knowledge and expertise
Authority	Leading others
Courage	Bravery; doing difficult things in moments of fear

If you are using note cards:

◆ First, sort these cards into three piles, designating your most important values, less important values, and least important values. Our priorities vary, so there is no judgment on these. Use presence and defusion if judgments arise.

◆ Next, select your pile of most important values. Re-sort this pile, and narrow it down to your top 10 most important values. Set aside the rest.

◆ Finally, pick up your top 10 values, and from these, select your top three values. Notice what it feels like to make this selection.

If you are using a journal:

◆ First, write a star next to the most important values, a circle next to the less important values, and an X next to the least important values. Again, priorities vary, so there is no judgment on these. Use presence and defusion if judgments arise.

◆ Next, rewrite the values with stars next to them. From these, star the 10 most important values.

◆ Finally, rewrite the starred values. Now choose your top three values. Notice what it feels like to make that decision.

Values Writing

MATERIALS: Timer or clock, journal
SUGGESTED TIME: 15 minutes

Values writing can help you freely identify values in an area of your life where you want to act. Spending time journaling about the most important areas of your life often identifies new paths forward.

- Choose an area of your life that is important to you, where you feel like you have not been living your values. For many of us, there is a sense of unease, anxiety, or disappointment around this. If you are having trouble identifying an area, here are some ideas:

Family	Community
Romantic relationships	Spirituality
Friendships	Learning/education
Recreation/fun	Physical health
Work/career	Environment
Parenting	Art, creativity, and beauty

- Set a timer for 15 minutes, and write freely about how you want to be in this area. Use the metaphors above. What direction do you want to go? How would you want people to toast you at a party for this? How would you want to be remembered in this area? When have you lived well in this area, and what were you doing at the time? Who are your role models in this area of life? What are they doing? Free write on this for the whole time.

- Read through what you read afterward, identifying values. Notice if goals or actions were also present, and note these. They might be helpful in the following chapter.

- Try to keep this area of your life present each day. Notice when you feel like you are living in a values-congruent way in this area.

Identifying Barriers to Valued Action

MATERIALS: Journal
SUGGESTED TIME: 5 to 10 minutes

You might remember from the rock metaphor that we can find values in the same places we find pain (see page 116). The reverse, of course, is also true. As we go toward our values, pain will show up. It can be helpful to identify that right away, and prepare skills or behaviors when those painful things arise. To borrow from our repeated metaphor, this exercise is about identifying potential passengers that come along for the ride when you steer your bus in your valued direction. This exercise will set you up for the next chapter, when you start to take action on your values.

◆ Start with identifying the value you want to live and writing it down. Take a few breaths and visualize yourself living this value over the next week. How will you be showing up in your life if you are living this value? What actions might you take? How would you be inter-acting with others? Notice what comes to mind.

◆ Write the thoughts and emotions that come to mind.

◆ Identify ways you might engage in avoidance. What are your "red flags" for moving away from values?

◆ Now identify defusion, acceptance, presence, and observing self skills to use for each set of experiences. Match these skills to each of the thoughts, emotions, and avoidance behaviors you have already identified.

◆ Ask yourself if you are willing to have these experiences in order to move toward that value. Remember that willingness is like taking a jump: You cannot jump halfway, but you can decide on the size of the jump. So, if the answer is no, consider whether there is a length of time or different task that would increase your willing-ness to experience these thoughts and feelings for this value.

Here's an example of identifying barriers:

Marcus valued contribution and hard work. When he visualized living those values, he imagined going back to school for an advanced degree, starting a nonprofit, and working to end inequality. He identified several thoughts and feelings that would come up and how he would handle them. They are laid out below.

MY VALUE: CONTRIBUTION AND HARD WORK

THOUGHTS: "You are going to fail." "You can't do this." "It is too hard." "Who do you think you are?" "You are a loser."
    SKILLS: *Name Your Mind, Thanking the Mind, mindfulness of thoughts, Blue Sky*

EMOTIONS: Fear, anxiety, rapid heartbeat, nausea, guilt, shame
    SKILLS: *Mindfulness of emotions, body scan, Blue Sky, Continuous You*

AVOIDANCE: Not signing up for classes, not attending classes, watching TV, smoking cannabis, arguing with girlfriend
    SKILLS: *Mindfulness of the present (Three-Breath Check-In), remembering my values*

I am willing to experience all these experiences in order to move toward my values. I commit to experiencing all this for at least five minutes before giving myself permission to start avoiding again.

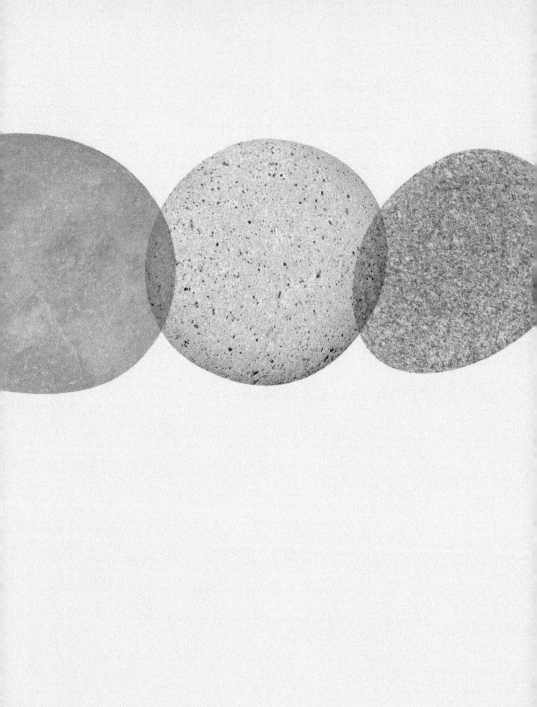

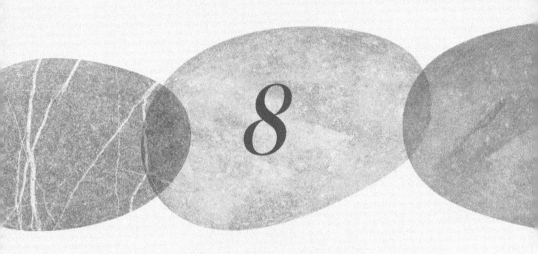

COMMITTED ACTION

Committed action is where you will see all the hard work and new skills you have learned put into practice toward building the full and meaningful life I have encouraged since chapter 1. Here is where you will take action and make more external changes. Know that old thoughts and emotions will come up as you do, so keep all the acceptance skills (defusion, acceptance, presence, and observing self) at the ready. Putting committed action into practice also asks us to practice presence, observing self, and connection with values. While this may look like the end of the book, this is truly only the beginning of your journey. Keep all six skill sets with you each day to continue living the life you want to live.

This chapter will cover committed action, what it looks like, and how to do it. Misconceptions and a case study will further deepen your understanding of committed action. Finally, exercises at the close of the chapter will help you put the skill into practice.

Behind the Method

Identifying our values can give us a sense of what is important to us and how to live a full life. If we stopped there, however, we would never *experience* that full life. Committed action is about putting our feet where our heart is; namely, taking steps that move us in line with our values. For many, identifying values leads to more questions, such as "How do I do this?" or "What now?" This chapter will help you explore those questions. Once you know next steps, it will also help you move forward and stay on the path.

Committed action in ACT is defined as any action that is based on a value, made at a certain moment in time, and linked to larger patterns of action. Commitment here is used to describe the moment we choose to act in alignment with a value. It is not a long-term promise. Committed action means taking moment-by-moment action associated with a value that builds upon itself. Because they are connected to values, these actions are reinforcing, thus leading us to do more and bigger actions associated with values. Commitment is not a one-time decision; it is inherently in the present, and something we decide every day.

Like values, committed action is freely chosen. There is no right or wrong choice. There is only choice and its outcome. You will almost definitely slip up and drop away from your values. At that point, you have two options: admit defeat and quit, or admit that you slipped and commit by taking a step toward your value. The latter will move you closer to your goals, but also requires you to experience painful emotions associated with slipping up.

Recall that values reflect what is most important to us. Without action, they remain just ideals. Action allows you to live your values, to receive the benefit of being true to what is most important to you. That is why we start with values. Too many of us know what it feels like to pick a goal, like getting a degree or a job, without it being attached to a specific value. We work and we work, and we wonder what we are working for. It all feels empty.

Alternatively, committed action puts that work toward something deeply important. We work and we work, and we know what we are working for. It also means that failures, disappointments, and setbacks are not catastrophic. They are just a point to recommit to our values. If there is something you feel you "have" to do, finding the value it might be associated with can give you more choice. Perhaps you are doing something in pursuit of your marriage, a value of helping others, or for your children. Linking to the value can turn a once dreaded activity to a choice, even when the same discomfort shows up.

Techniques for Committed Action

The following techniques include metaphors for how to understand committed action as well as ways to implement that action.

Leader of a Nonprofit

Imagine that you are the leader of a nonprofit. You have been in this role for a few months now and under your command, the organization has been excelling. What would happen if you left your job? It is easy to imagine that the progress that you worked for would reverse. Similarly, stopping skills as you see progress will likely result in moving back into fusion and avoidance. Now imagine that as things get difficult, you take a job with another nonprofit. You might see progress again, but eventually things will get difficult. Instead, staying at this organization may mean experiencing difficulties, but sticking with it can result in greater meaning and connection. Furthermore, in this context, sending emails and completing forms is more than just administrative tasks, but part of a larger effort to change people's lives. Similarly, we need to keep taking action with our values to see any long-term benefits.

Passengers on the Bus (Final Edition)

We've arrived at the final stop of our Passengers on the Bus meta-phor (see page 50). Recall that passengers represent thoughts and feelings, and values are the direction you want to go. Committed action is the act of driving in the direction you want. It is the act of moving the steering wheel and accelerating the vehicle.

Waiting for the Wrong Cab

We often make deals with ourselves, like "I will take action when I feel less anxious. I will speak up when I feel confident." It is a bit like going out and calling a cab. Two cabs arrive; one is sparkly and clean with the latest technology, and the other is an older car that has not seen a car wash. You want to take the new cab, but the driver is on break. Meanwhile, the driver of the older cab is picking up passengers and leaving. And then another shabby cab comes by, picking up more passengers, while you continue to wait. You could keep waiting for your chosen driver to get off break, or you could jump in the next car that arrives and get where you want to go.

Tiniest Step

Sometimes committed action brings up fear of failure. The word commitment can evoke thoughts of forever and perfection. If you find yourself stuck in this way, taking a tiny step can help you expe-rience the power of committed action without as much baggage. It is also helpful when moving toward a value has a lot of pain, such as seeking connection after a lifetime of rejection.

Identify the value you want to live, and pick one small thing you can do in the next 24 hours. If health is a value, it might mean taking a walk around the block. If connection is a value, calling an old friend or family member might be a tiny step. If launching a blog or getting published are goals within the value of creation, start by writing 500 words.

Just Because

In *A Liberated Mind*, Dr. Steven C. Hayes writes about abstaining from dessert for a year—"just because." It was not linked to specific value; he just knew it was difficult and wanted to see if he could do it. Similarly, pick something that might challenge you and commit to it—just because. We are so used to reasons, rules, and "should"s dominating our actions. "Just because" allows you to use choice to guide your actions. Taking the stairs does not need to be for fitness or the "right" thing to do. It can be just because.

Thomas Takes Committed Action

Thomas started working with me on anxiety following the dissolution of a relationship. As we worked on acceptance skills, we also identified values and committed action steps. The fluidity of these actions week to week is an excellent case study of committed action.

Thomas and I identified two important values that he wanted to nurture: self-respect, which he defined as setting boundaries in a compassionate and authentic way, and health. When anxiety showed up, it was easy for him to eat too much, not exercise, and neglect sleep. Early on, committed action meant practicing workable sleep patterns: getting in bed before 11 p.m., keeping electronics out of the room and reading a physical book to wind down, practicing gentle yoga or meditating in the hour before sleep, and not taking naps during the day. When he noticed himself scrolling through social media in bed, he recommitted by getting present with fear and sadness and choosing to put his phone outside the room. As those practices improved Thomas's sleep, he began committing to physical activity. Some days that meant a walk around the block. Thomas practiced defusion when self-critical thoughts appeared, telling him that he needed to do more.

As Thomas practiced defusion, acceptance, and presence skills, he was more able to watch the urges to eat, and notice when they were driven by fears or by a desire to be soothed. He could practice self-compassion and presence, or take a walk to accept these emotions without eating to soothe them. He found it easier to tune into his body's needs, and to eat only when and what his body wanted. He still enjoyed daily coffee and treats; he was just not beholden to his mind's every urge and desire. He even found himself eating more vegetables! After defusing from thoughts that he "deserved" or "needed" sweet foods after a long day, more options opened up.

As Thomas made these commitments and practiced these skills, he found himself setting boundaries with people who mistreated him. In some relationships, that meant vocalizing how a comment hurt him and making a request for a different behavior. In other relationships, it meant limiting communication altogether. He discovered the friendships that he valued and nurtured those, even when fear of rejection showed up.

Thomas's experience demonstrates how committed action leads to larger and larger patterns of behavior. If I asked Thomas to start sleeping better, exercising daily, and asserting himself in his relationships at the start of therapy, he likely would have been flooded with fear and, quite reasonably, anger at me for making such large demands. Yet we often demand similarly heroic acts from ourselves! Instead, Thomas practiced acceptance skills as he took manageable steps each day toward what was important. Some days the steps felt too small and other days it took effort and willingness to experience pain to take the steps. He found that by setting moderately easy steps in the beginning, he was able to gain some momentum.

Misconceptions

Remember that committed action is not about making a future promise. It is about stepping toward your value right here, right now. We recommit to our values each day. As Thomas experienced, some days find us with a lot of pain and very noisy passengers. Because he identified reasonable committed action beforehand, he was able to use defusion, acceptance, presence, and observing self skills to reorient to his commitment for the day.

Committed action is values based, so it is not emotion based. Our emotions often set our goals and limits. When we get anxious, we stop, and when we feel better, we proceed. Committed action asks that we take the steps no matter how we feel. Remember that willingness is a bit like jumping. You cannot make a half jump. You either jump or you do not, but you do get to decide how *big* a jump to make. You can choose the extent of your committed action with a willingness to experience whatever comes with it. Someone with agoraphobia might decide to walk in a mall for 10 minutes before giving themselves permission to go back to the car. They are not setting a limit on the emotions or sensations they will feel; they are simply setting a limit on how long they will be in the mall. An exercise below will help you work with your own willingness.

These exercises will help you begin to identify committed actions so that you can get out there and start fully living your life!

SMART Goals with Values

MATERIALS: Journal
SUGGESTED TIME: Varies

SMART goals are helpful because they provide the information that supports us in following through with action. Even SMART goals are empty, however, without connection to a value. You'll now create a SMART goal directly related to one of your values. I will provide an example below to demonstrate how these steps play out.

SMART is an acronym for goals with specific features:

» SPECIFIC: Identifies the behavior, frequency, duration, and place

» MEASURABLE: Provides criteria for knowing when the goal is reached

» ATTAINABLE: Reasonable for your current ability and resources

» RELEVANT: Related to your value

» TIMELY: Has an end point to assess progress

1. Using your journal, identify the value you want to nurture and live by over the next week. If you need help with this, return to the exercises in chapter 7. Consider using one of the values you identified in the values sorting exercise.

2. Identify a long-term goal: This goal might take a year or two to accomplish. Write it down in a sentence or two.

3. Now, create a SMART goal based on that. What do you specifically want to accomplish? How will you know when you have accomplished this goal? When do you want to check in on progress? Remember to ask yourself if it is related to your value and not too challenging.

Continued

EXERCISE

4. Next, create a medium-term goal using SMART goal criteria. This one might take the next six months to accomplish. Be sure to be quite specific with what you want to do in this time frame.

5. Finally, write a short-term goal in SMART format. This might only take a week to a month.

6. Look at that last goal and sit in silence for a moment, noticing what comes up. What is your mind saying about the goal? What do you feel in your body about this goal? Observe these experiences from the perspective of your observing self.

7. If, after completing this exercise, you find yourself wanting to add a shorter-term goal to complete in the coming days, or another medium-term goal, complete the SMART criteria again. Also notice if any of your goals are unrealistic. Use defusion techniques and observing skills. Defuse from thoughts like "I can't do this," but be realistic. Defusion skills can help you become unstuck from thoughts, and intentionally decide their helpfulness.

Here is Sasha's example.

She values art, learning, and helping others, and wants to use art to champion for social causes. However, anxiety about being good enough shows up to such a degree that she struggles to complete art classes.

VALUE: Creativity, Learning, Contributing

GENERAL GOAL: I want to complete my art degree and teach art classes to support vulnerable groups.

> *[These goals are big! That is great. The problem is that it is hard for Sasha to know how to reach them, or when she will accomplish them. Making these goals SMART will help Sasha move forward.]*

LONG-TERM SMART GOAL: Complete the remaining 45 credits of art school in four semesters.

> *[Notice that identifying remaining credits makes this goal **specific, measurable**, and **timely** by setting the four-semester time frame. Sasha knows that she could complete these credits in three semesters, but added another semester to make this goal more **realistic** and **attainable**]*

MEDIUM-TERM GOAL: Have three finished art pieces for class by the end of the semester.

> *[Sasha might get even more specific by identifying the size of these pieces. Three small pieces may be realistic, but three large pieces might be unattainable in that time frame. She might also determine if the pieces will relate to each other somehow. Looking at her class's expectations can help answer these questions.]*

MEDIUM-TERM GOAL: To learn how to teach art in ways that support social causes, I will meet with community leaders in the communities I want to serve, for conversations about how art could support them. I will have two meetings in the next four months and will also meet with a current art teacher within that time frame to gather information.

[This goal demonstrates how to make a SMART goal with an as-yet-unidentified outcome. Sasha knows she wants to combine art and social advocacy, but isn't sure what that will look like yet. This goal clearly outlines how she can gather that information in a timely manner. It also gives her smaller, specific steps that can inform her short-term goals ahead.]

SHORT-TERM GOAL: Complete upcoming art project for class by next Thursday. I will use Name Your Mind, mindfulness of emotions, and Blue Sky to work with anxiety and perfectionism.

SHORT-TERM GOAL: Email my mentor to ask to set up a meeting in the next two weeks. Email a leader of a community group in the next month.

[Sasha knows that perfectionism and anxiety will show up when she does this project, so she is already outlining which skills she needs. The last goal is more medium-term but demonstrates how larger goals can be broken up into smaller goals.]

Willingness Jumps

MATERIALS: Journal
SUGGESTED TIME: Varies

Willingness—defined as our ability to hold whatever internal experience shows up without avoiding, opting out, or leaving—is key to committed action. We often make deals with ourselves, e.g., "I will take action when I feel less anxious." Willingness asks if you are willing to take action right now, with anxiety present.

For this exercise, answer these questions first by sitting quietly with them, then by recording them in your journal.

- To start, get in an alert but comfortable position. Take a few breaths, noticing your breathing. Notice sensations of sitting.

- When you notice that you are present, sit with each question for a few breaths.

- What is the value you want to embody in the coming days?

- Notice what comes up for you, both in thoughts and in emotions.

- Briefly note that in your journal.

- Return to your sitting position and take a few breaths to become present again.

- If anxiety disappeared today, how would you embody that value? Close your eyes and visualize your actions. What do you feel and see when you embody that action? Return to this after you have a vibrant sense of how you would act.

- Record some notes in your journal about how you most want to act.

Continued

- Return to your sitting position and take a few breaths to become present again.

- Again, visualize what you would do that embodies this value. This time, ask yourself what you would have to experience in pursuit of this action? What are the thoughts, emotions, sensations? How intense are they?

- Write these down as barriers in your journal. Return to sitting and get present again.

- Now ask yourself: Am I 100 percent willing to experience that right now in pursuit of that value in that action?

- If the answer is yes, then you are ready to start acting! Write down skills that you will want to use to practice willingness.

- If the answer is no, then diving in will likely lead to avoidance or opting-out. If you noticed a strong "NO" showing up, then let's continue.

- Ask yourself what kind of jump you would be 100 percent willing to do, even if anxiety showed up. How long would you be in the situation before giving yourself permission to leave? How much would you do to start?

- Once you have identified your "jump," visualize yourself taking that action. Notice what thoughts, emotions, and experiences come up.

- Write down the jump as well as the barriers that you felt visualizing the jump, then return to the present.

- Which skills will help you stay present and accepting of what comes along?

- Write those down, too.

Let's look at what Matt identified when he did a similar exercise.

The values I want to embody this week are "PRESENT AND ENGAGED."

If anxiety disappeared, I would be present and engaged with my children during the day, taking time to play with them and share joy. I would also be present and engaged with this difficult work project. I would research and write for a couple hours a day.

BARRIERS WHEN WORKING:

- ▸ THOUGHTS: My boss will hate this. This is garbage. I am a terrible writer.

- ▸ EMOTIONS/SENSATIONS: Urge to distract, panic in my chest, tightness in my throat, nervous energy throughout my limbs, discomfort in sitting still

- ▸ BEHAVIORS: Getting up, distracting myself, opening another tab on my browser to go to social media

Am I 100 percent willing to experience all this in pursuit of my work: NO.

BARRIERS WHEN PLAYING WITH MY CHILDREN:

- ▸ THOUGHTS: I should be working. I don't do this enough. What if my kids resent me?

- ▸ EMOTIONS/SENSATIONS: Guilt and shame, urge to overcompensate and play more, sadness at them growing up

- ▸ BEHAVIORS: Playing with them with my mind elsewhere, not fully engaged

Am I 100 percent willing to experience all this to play with my kids: YES.

SKILLS NEEDED: Staying present, focusing on my children's facial expressions and words, observing self to witness the play, my own joy, and my children's joy

What behavior associated with work am I 100 percent willing to do if anxiety shows up?

- ‣ I am willing to work on the project for five minutes with all those experiences showing up.

- ‣ SKILLS: I will use defusion (Name Your Mind, page 43) and observing self to stay present.

- ‣ After five minutes, I give myself permission to take a break, and could continue working if I choose to.

Matt used these commitments—engaging fully with his children throughout the day and engaging fully with work for at least five minutes—throughout the week after completing this exercise. He found that by practicing willingness and commitment, he was able to work on his project for longer and longer, eventually working on it for an hour at a time before playing with his children. After two weeks of this action, he reported that he had never felt so present with both work and his children.

Troubleshooting Failures

MATERIALS: Journal
SUGGESTED TIME: Varies

We will inevitably move away from our values and not complete committed action. At that point we can quit or recommit—that's it. Those are our two options. This exercise will help you recommit and identify ways to continue moving forward. Reflecting on what got in the way of your committed action can be helpful in preventing the same barriers from disrupting you again.

◆ Identify the behavior you were trying to do, and what happened. Try to be detailed, writing what you were thinking and feeling to the best of your memory.

◆ From there, identify barriers and categorize them in the following list:

FUSION: Thoughts or rules I fused with

AVOIDANCE: Emotions or experiences I did not want to feel

> *Opting out? Distracting? Habitually forgetting? Putting it off indefinitely?*

LOGISTICAL BARRIERS: External problems that need to be solved

> *Be careful of this. Our minds often create external barriers to justify experiential avoidance. Notice if logistical barriers keep coming up and see if they are hiding avoidance.*

NOT SMART: Were your goals unattainable or impossible to measure? Were they relevant to your value?

◆ Now, looking at your barriers, identify next steps. Do you need to change your goal to make it more SMART? Do you need to problem solve a logistical barrier? Do you need to identify skills to practice acceptance and defusion? List these out.

Alex completed this exercise after not following through on a goal to exercise every day.

BEHAVIOR: EXERCISE EVERY DAY

BARRIERS

- ▸ FUSION: I am too tired. I can't do this. I am sore. I don't want to.
- ▸ AVOIDANCE: Feelings of tiredness and lethargy
- ▸ LOGISTICAL BARRIERS: None (I have all the necessary equipment, like walking shoes and a pair of dumbbells).
- ▸ SMART: The goal may have been unattainable because I went from not exercising for years to exercising daily.
- ▸ NEW PLAN: I will exercise for 30 minutes, 3 times a week for 2 weeks.

Alex's new goal allowed her to start more slowly and check in two weeks later on changing her goal.

A Final Word

Although this is the end of this book, it is only the beginning of your journey. In Getting Started (see page xii), I compared learning ACT to learning to ride a bike. You are now prepared to cruise around town, changing your relationship to anxiety with all the skills you have acquired. Hopefully you feel more empowered, and anxiety is holding you back less from the life you want to live.

If you continue practicing these skills, you will likely notice a shift in your approach to anxiety. You will find yourself using these skills in more natural ways as you go, and notice yourself taking steps that seemed like dreams just a few months ago. Continue practicing, and if you notice yourself struggling with anxiety, return to practice any of the exercises in this book. Also, know that if you can notice that you are currently struggling with anxiety, you are practicing presence! That is progress.

Be kind to yourself. Learning to stop making enemies of our emotions and thoughts takes work and practice. However, this practice and work opens you up to the world. It allows you to learn from yourself, to work toward your deepest dreams, and to connect with others. When we stop living in fear and step into courage, we have more power than we could have ever imagined. Also, recognize that community and connection are vital to all of us. As a result, using these skills will move you closer to finding people you can share yourself with, allowing you to find joy, meaning, and closeness.

This work is lifelong. As long as our minds are active, the fusion and avoidance processes will be, too. The good news is that the practice of psychological flexibility is now available and present for you as well. Every day, the choice between fusion and avoidance or psychological flexibility will be there. I wish you the best in this lifelong path from suffering to healing, as ACT allows you "act," and to have compassion for yourself and others along the way.

Resources

A Liberated Mind by Dr. Steven C. Hayes: The originator of ACT wrote this book in 2019 about ACT skills and the research. Nearly 15 years in the making, it is one of the best resources for learning more about ACT.

Be Mighty by Jill Stoddard: This terrific book applies ACT to common experiences among women.

Portland Psychotherapy: Wonderful ACT therapists and researchers Jenna LeJeune and Jason Luoma offer digital resources at their Oregon clinic's website, PortlandPsychotherapy.com/resources /acceptance_and_commitment_therapy_exercises_and_audiofiles.

The Association for Contextual Behavioral Science (ACBS): This organization offers an online registry to choose the ACT therapist to help you along your journey, at ContextualScience.org/tips_for _seeking_therapist. They also offer a resource to find books applying ACT to specific concerns, from relationships to OCD to depression, at ContextualScience.org/act_books_self_help.

Headspace app: This app teaches mindfulness based on the Buddhist tradition. It works very well with ACT. Find more info at Headspace.com.

References

American Psychiatric Association. *Diagnostic and Statistical Manual of Mental Disorders, Fifth Edition.* Arlington, VA: American Psychiatric Association, 2013.

American Psychological Association. "Stress Effects on the Body." November 1, 2018. apa.org/helpcenter/stress-body.

Bandelow, Borwin and Sophie Michaelis. "Epidemiology of Anxiety Disorders in the 21st Century." *Dialogues in Clinical Neuroscience* 17, no. 3 (September 2015): 327–335. ncbi.nlm.nih.gov/pmc/articles /PMC4610617.

Barlow, David H. *Clinical Handbook of Psychological Disorders: A Step-by-Step Treatment Manual.* 5th ed. New York, NY: The Guilford Press, 2014.

Booth, Robert. "Master of Mindfulness, Jon Kabat-Zinn: 'People Are Losing Their Minds. This Is What We Need to Wake Up To.'" *Guardian*, October 22, 2017. theguardian.com/lifeandstyle/2017 /oct/22/mindfulness-jon-kabat-zinn-depression-trump-grenfell.

Cozolino, Louis. *The Neuroscience of Psychotherapy: Healing the Social Brain.* 2nd ed. New York, NY: W.W. Norton & Company, 2010.

Davis, Martha, Elizabeth Robbins Eshelman, and Matthew McKay. *The Relaxation and Stress Reduction Workbook.* 6th ed. Oakland, CA: New Harbinger Publications, 2008.

Dillner, Luisa. "Is There Any Benefit to Daydreaming?" *Guardian*, November 6, 2017. theguardian.com/lifeandstyle/2017/nov/06/is -any-benefit-to-daydreaming-mind-wandering-useful-function.

Eifert, Georg H. and John Forsyth. *Acceptance and Commitment Therapy for Anxiety Disorders.* Oakland, CA: New Harbinger Publications, 2005.

Harris, Russ. *ACT Made Simple: An Easy-to-Read Primer on Acceptance and Commitment Therapy.* Oakland, CA: New Harbinger Publications, 2009.

Hayes, Steven C. *A Liberated Mind: How to Pivot Toward What Matters*. New York, NY: Avery, 2019.

LeJeune, Jenna, and Jason Luoma. *Seven Values "Greatest Hits": Our Favorite Values Exercises from Acceptance and Commitment Therapy*. Portland Psychotherapy, 2016. portlandpsychotherapytraining.com /wp-content/uploads/sites/22/2016/06/Favorite_act_values_exercise _scripts.pdf.

———. *Values in Therapy: A Clinician's Guide to Helping Clients Explore Values, Increase Psychological Flexibility & Live a More Meaningful Life*. Oakland, CA: Context Press, 2019.

Linehan, Marsha M. *Cognitive-Behavioral Treatment of Borderline Personality Disorder*. New York, NY: The Guilford Press, 1993.

———. "Emotion Regulation Skills," in *DBT Skills Training Manual*. New York, NY: The Guilford Press, 2015.

Healing and the Mind, episode 3, "Healing from Within." Directed by Kate Tapley, hosted by Bill Moyers. Aired February 23, 1993, on PBS. billmoyers.com/content/healing-from-within.

Neff, Kristen. "Exercise 2: Self-Compassion Break." Self-Compassion. Last modified December 13, 2015. https://self-compassion.org /exercise-2-self-compassion-break.

Newman, Michelle G., Sandra J. Llera, Thane Erickson, Amy Przeworski, and Louis Gastonguay. "Worry and Generalized Anxiety Disorder: A Review and Theoretical Synthesis of Evidence on Nature, Etiology, Mechanisms, and Treatment." *Annual Review of Clinical Psychology* 9 (2013): 275–297. doi.org/10.1146 /annurev-clinpsy-050212-185544.

Patriquin, Michelle A., and Sanjay J. Mathew. "The Neurobiological Mechanisms of Generalized Anxiety Disorder and Chronic Stress." *Chronic Stress* 1 (2017): 1–10. doi.org/10.1177/2470547017703993.

Steimer, Thierry. "The Biology of Fear- and Anxiety-Related Behaviors." *Dialogues in Clinical Neuroscience* 4, no. 3 (2002): 231–249.

Stoddard, Jill A., and Niloofar Afari. *The Big Book of ACT Metaphors: A Practitioner's Guide to Experiential Exercises and Metaphors in Acceptance and Commitment Therapy.* Oakland, CA: New Harbinger Publications, 2014.

Törneke, Niklas. *Learning RFT: An Introduction to Relational Frame Theory and Its Clinical Application.* Oakland, CA: Context Press, 2010.

Index

A

Acceptance
  acceptance
    techniques, 64–66
  in the ACT context, 22–23,
    29, 62, 112
  as an ACT skill, 45, 78, 99,
    116, 128, 132–133, 134
  defining, 34, 58
  defusion, adding
    acceptance skills to, 46
  identifying skills to
    practice acceptance, 143
  misconceptions,
    awareness of, 67–68
  self-acceptance,
    cultivating through the
    observing self, 95–96
  third wave behavior
    treatments, used
    with, 20
  willingness as a
    synonym for, 59
Acceptance in ACT
    exercises
  Acceptance
    Meditation, 69–70
  Body Scan Meditation, 90
  Drop the Rope, 64
  Identify
    Willingness, 71–72

Identifying Barriers to
    Valued Action, 124
  Looking for a
    Passenger, 73
  Observing with
    Compassion, 108
  Saying Yes, 65
Acceptance and
    Commitment
    Therapy (ACT)
  components of, 22–24
  language theory in, 26–27
  Leaves on a Stream as a
    classic exercise of, 53
  mindfulness in the ACT
    approach, 24–25
  origins of, 19–20
  Passengers on the
    Bus as an original
    metaphor of, 50
  as a process-based
    treatment, 3, 12
  psychological flexibility as
    goal of, 21
  suffering, viewing as a
    normal process, 3, 18
  symbolic thought,
    reducing the
    power of, 28
  workability as the guiding
    litmus test in, 35, 39

Acknowledgments

We are all standing on the shoulders of giants, and I am so lucky for the giants in my life.

Thank you to the entire team at Callisto Media for choosing an unknown author for this project and for being the best team to work with.

Thank you to Steven C. Hayes, Kelly Wilson, and Kirk Strosahl for giving the world your research. You have changed the course of humanity.

Deep appreciation to the ACBS community: Seeing thousands of people collaborate, support each other, and be vulnerable together gives me hope for our future.

A special thanks to my own ACT community, including my lovely writing group. I also want to thank my Bay Area therapist friends and consultation groups. I am so grateful for all of you.

To the village of therapists who built me: thank you, Jennifer Villatte, for being the first ACT therapist I encountered. I remember your warmth most of all. Thank you to Jacqueline Pistorello for your mentorship, compassion, and laughs. Thank you to Casey Kohl and Jodi Thomas for your mentorship and for making me feel whole; you may never know how much your faith in me has meant. Thank you to Tom Embree for the support and care you have given me. It has changed my life. And thank you for sitting with me when I cried, "If I am not my thoughts, what am I?!"

Thank you to Jade and Maria, the best friends a girl could ask for.

To my family: Thank you, Mom, for seeing me in a different light on my darkest days; thank you, Dad, for believing in great things for me; and finally to Troy: I am so glad to have you by my side in this great adventure.

Finally, to my clients: I have deep appreciation to all of you for what you have taught me about the human condition. Walking along your life path, however briefly, has been an honor.

About the Author

RACHEL WILLIMOTT, LCSW, has a private practice located in the San Francisco Bay Area. She has a psychology degree from the University of Nevada, Reno (UNR), and a master's in social work with a mental health emphasis from the University of Southern California. After learning about ACT at UNR, she returned there for her clinical internship. When she discovered that an entire career could be dedicated to learning about people, listening deeply, and having important conversations, she knew that was what she wanted to do. For more information about her private practice, visit www.rachelwlcsw.com.

Rachel now lives in Oakland, California, and enjoys spending time with her husband, sweet cat, and fearful dog. You might find her hiking in the woods or breathing in the ocean air.

CPSIA information can be obtained
at www.ICGtesting.com
Printed in the USA
LVHW020044071120
670934LV00003B/4

9 781647 398644